GERONTOLOGICAL SOCIAL WORK SUPERVISION

Ann Burack-Weiss, DSW
Francis Coyle Brennan, ACSW

SOME ADVANCE REVIEWS

"Burack-Weiss and Brennan's book provides a wonderful and much needed resource for new and veteran social workers doing supervision in long-term care programs and community agencies. The authors effectively identify the particular demands of gerontological social work based on their long experiences as supervisors and educators. The book is rich in practice guidelines that are readily translated into reflective and humane approaches to supervision and gerontological practice."

George Getzel, DSW
Professor, Hunter College School of Social Work

"This is a lively book, replete with vivid, engaging vignettes and creative ideas to aid supervisors working both with student and experienced social workers in the field of aging. Agency administrative realities are refreshingly spelled out. Client accountability and outcomes must supersede educational concerns. A supervisor must concentrate his or her efforts on the workers' use of time and assessment of needs. In this dark period of reduced agency budgets, especially in aging, these are welcome, helpful words."

Lucy Rosengarten, ACSW
Founder and General Manager of COHME, Inc.
(Concerned Home Managers for the Elderly, Inc.)
New York, NY

Gerontological Social Work Supervision

HAWORTH Social Work Practice
Carlton Munson, Senior Editor

New, Recent and Forthcoming Titles

Management and Information Systems in Human Services: Implications for the Distribution of Authority and Decision Making by Richard K. Caputo

The Creative Practitioner: Creative Theory and Method for the Helping Services by Bernard Gelfand

Social Work Theory and Practice with the Terminally Ill by Joan K. Parry, DSW

Social Work in Health Settings: Practice in Context by Toba Schwaber Kerson and Associates

Gerontological Social Work Supervision by Ann Burack-Weiss and Frances Coyle Brennan

Group Work: Skills and Strategies for Effective Interventions by Sondra Brandler and Camille P. Roman

If a Partner Has AIDS: Guide to Clinical Intervention for Relationships in Crisis by R. Dennis Shelby

Social Work Practice: A Systems Approach by Benyamin Chetkow-Yanoov

Elements of the Helping Process: A Guide for Clinicians by Raymond Fox

Gerontological Social Work Supervision

Ann Burack-Weiss
Frances Coyle Brennan

The Haworth Press
New York • London • Sydney

The Haworth Press, Inc., 10 Alice Street, Binghamton, NY 13904-1580
EUROSPAN/Haworth, 3 Henrietta Street, London WC2E 8LU England
ASTAM/Haworth, 162-168 Parramatta Road, Stanmore, Sydney, N.S.W. 2048 Australia

Library of Congress Cataloging-in-Publication Data

Burack-Weiss, Ann.
    Gerontological social work supervision / Ann Burack-Weiss, Frances Coyle Brennan.
      p. cm.
    Includes bibliographical references and index.
    ISBN 0-86656-827-1 (acid-free paper) — ISBN 1-56024-182-9 (pbk. : alk. paper)
    1. Social work with the aged—United States. 2. Supervision of social workers—United States. I. Brennan, Frances Coyle. II Title.
HV1465.B87 1991
362.6'068'3—dc20
                                                        91-339
                                                        CIP

CONTENTS

PART III: EDUCATIONAL AND ADMINISTRATIVE SUPERVISION

ABOUT THE AUTHORS

Ann Burack-Weiss, DSW, is currently Adjunct Associate Professor at the Columbia University School of Social Work in New York City. She is also an independent consultant on staff training and program development to many social agencies. Her gerontological experience spans two decades and has included practice, supervisory, and administrative positions at the Community Service Society, the Jewish Home and Hospital for Aged in New York City, and in private practice. She is the co-author of three books and the author of numerous papers on long-term care, case management, clinical assessment and intervention with older persons, family care giving, and social work education. She has conducted work-shops throughout the country for the National Council on Aging and the American Society on Aging and has been a guest lecturer at the Paul Baerwald School of Social Work at Hebrew University in Jerusalem. Dr. Burack-Weiss is a recipient of the National Association of Social Workers (NASW) New York City Chapter's 1989 Social Worker in Aging Award.

Frances Coyle Brennan, ACSW, is Associate Director, Department of Social Service, at the Jewish Home and Hospital for Aged in New York City. Previously she was associated with the Jewish Home and Hospital for Aged at the Kingsbridge Division. Her past experience includes a year as Adjunct Lecturer in Social Work at the Columbia University School of Social Work. The co-author of the book *First Encounters Between Elders and Agencies: A Practice Guide*, she has extensive supervisory and administrative experience in serving the elderly in community and institutional settings.

Acknowledgements

Completion of a book is a time of remembrance and gratitude. Our first acknowledgement is to the countless gerontological social work supervisors in the New York City area with whom we have worked over the past two decades. Some of them were first-time agency field instructors. Others were experienced field instructors or educational coordinators. Some of them supervised one or two practitioners while others administered large social service agencies or departments in health care organizations. All struggled to find a way to integrate generic principles of supervision with specific gerontological applications. And, as their consultants and faculty field advisors, we struggled along with them. This book reflects their practice problems and practice wisdom. Our thanks are, foremost, to them.

Next we acknowledge our readers: Susannah Chandler, Rose Goldstein, and Seena Freedman made valuable suggestions on the work in progress. Special thanks are due to Diane Livingston for the substantive and editorial comments that enhanced our second draft.

At The Columbia University School of Social Work, we thank the field work department and Seminar in Field Instructor participants and faculty. The section on Educational Supervision is indebted to them. A special thank you to Rose Dobrof for encouragement at the outset of this project. At the Jewish Home and Hospital for Aged, we thank Dr. Natalie Gordon for her support and encouragement.

Time for writing a book is time away from families. To Roy Weiss and Tom Brennan who now know more about the making of a book than they ever wished to; to Caroline and Tommy Brennan who may one day write their own books; to Donna and Rick Nelson and Kenneth Weiss for whom books open the talents of hands and heart; to Danielle Nelson who likes to turn pages, we dedicate our book with deepest love.

PART I
AN OVERVIEW

Chapter 1

Principles of Gerontological Social Work Practice

INTRODUCTION

Why a Book on Gerontological Social Work Supervision?

For over a decade we have supervised, consulted with, and trained social workers in practice with the aging. During that time, we looked in vain for the literature that would offer us guidance. Finding none, we extrapolated from generic texts on supervision, literature on aging, and unpublished practice and supervisory wisdom of colleagues in the field.

Sometimes it all came together. Sometimes it did not. When it did, we could effectively prepare a young student, whose only previous exposure to aging was a globe-trotting grandmother, to enter a nursing home unit of Alzheimer's patients. When it did not, we were unable to help a middle-aged senior worker recognize that her identification with an adult daughter was distorting her assessment of an elderly couple's care needs.

In time, we were scoring more hits than misses. Clearly, there *was* something different about supervising practice with the aging, but exactly what? Was it merely that generic texts on supervision lacked case examples of gerontological practice, or something more?

We began writing this book without answers to that question. We reasoned that even if case examples of older people were sufficient to flesh out time honored supervisory principles, that in itself would provide justification for a new book. The rise in the elderly population and the increase in services to meet their needs are bringing thousands of new workers into agencies serving the aged each year. Social work supervisors with experience in other fields of practice are being called upon to administer and train staff in programs for older persons. Master's level social workers in aging are moving into supervisory positions within a year or two of graduation. Often, they have not conceptualized practice for themselves, much less thought about how to convey it to others.

So we began to write and, in the process, to discover something more. What makes supervising gerontological practice different is that the clients served not only *could* be, but *will* be, us. While other populations can arouse the compassion and even the identification of social workers, it is not the same. The social and health problems faced by other populations are disturbances in the natural course of events, anomalies of the human condition. Aging *is* the natural course of events, the human condition. Social work students and workers may never know a schizophrenic, a substance abuser, or a developmentally disabled child outside of their professional work. But they will one day, if not today, be personally confronted with the issues that face their clients, both within their own families and for themselves. Supervision assumes an added dimension — that of helping workers use their deepest human connection with aged clients and their families to the best professional end.

At the same time, social work with the aging has similarities with other fields of practice. Most specifically, there is a dual emphasis on the person and environment and the blend of concrete and counselling services. Present in gerontological social work practice is the enabling role that empowers clients to help themselves, a mediating role that unites agency services with client needs, and an advocacy role to obtain needed resources.

Therefore, throughout this book, we will attempt to enhance the usefulness of generic principles with gerontological examples. We will also highlight where, when, and how the nature of the aging population makes a difference.

The Knowledge Base

Our knowledge base is grounded in two distinct bodies of literature: social work supervision and gerontological social work.

In social work supervision we are indebted to past and recent theoreticians. From the works of Reynolds and Towle, we incorporate the philosophical and psychodynamic roots of supervision. These early works on supervision remind us that the supervisee is a person with unique characteristics and life experiences. They alert us to the need for individualization, respect for learning style and awareness of the sequential stages of the learning process. Inductively based on these writers' own professional experiences, the supervisory principles imbedded in these works have a timeless truth that outlasts the agency services on which they were based.

The current literature on supervision is more often empirically based and cognizant of the impact of the agency's organizational structure on practice. Here, we have drawn most frequently on the works of Kadushin, Munson, and Shulman. They have helped us to identify what is indeed generic to all good supervisory practice and what must be modified to meet the needs of specific agencies and populations. Appendix A lists useful works on social work supervision.

In gerontological social work, we draw upon a vast and rapidly expanding body of knowledge, more readily categorized by subject matter than by author. This text assumes some gerontological knowledge and experience with aging on the part of the supervisor. Appendix B is a selective listing of books and journal articles on gerontological practice theory and techniques we have found useful for supervisors, workers, and students alike.

The Skills Base

The skills base of this text is unabashedly generic. From the interviewing skills of engagement, exploration, confrontation, clarification et al. to the conceptual skills of assessment and case planning — all are used equally by workers with aged clients and by supervisors with supervisees. Sometimes methods must be tailored to fit the individual situation. For example, the cognitively or sensorially impaired elder requires different engagement techniques than the mentally intact; the very young student requires different explanations than her more mature counterpart. But overall, these tools of the trade of the social work profession travel well.

About the Book

Part I (Chapters 1-3) provides a framework for approaching gerontological social work supervision, as well as an overview of gerontological practice and principles. This section presents the stages and styles of helping, learning, and teaching.

Part II (Chapters 4-5) discusses the teaching of practice skills, applicable to both educational and administrative supervision. We illustrate work with individuals, families, groups, interdisciplinary collaboration, and special issues.

Part III (Chapters 6-7) looks separately at educational and administrative supervision. In fact, these divisions are arbitrary. Differences are more of degree than of kind. Learning and doing go hand in hand from the first day of a student's field work placement to the last work day of a long professional career. If in educational supervision the emphasis is on learning, we must not forget the work that is its purpose and result. If in administrative supervision the emphasis is on task accomplishment, we must not forget that development of knowledge and skills is a never-ending process. Thus, we hope that the book will be read in its entirety by both educational and administrative supervisors.

Chapter 6 addresses educational supervision. The two-year Master's program is the model used throughout (i.e., the use of four semester evaluation criteria as a basis for teaching content). However, the principles may be adapted to the supervision of Bachelor's level students as well.

Chapter 7 addresses administrative supervision. It looks at differentials of organizational context and site as they influence social worker performance expectation and supervisory strategies.

PRINCIPLES OF GERONTOLOGICAL SOCIAL WORK

Gerontological social work is based on commonly held principles about the goals and processes of practice with the elderly. We share many of these with other health care providers. Here we discuss how the principles are manifested in the daily practice of social workers and the imperatives posed for supervisors.

Seeking Strengths

It is easy enough to identify the losses of older people—the diminished capacities and limited resources that cause them to seek help. It is more difficult and important to identify assets. Agencies and funding sources require documentation of problems to justify the provision of services. However, the gerontological social worker must seek out and mobilize a client's strengths.

The capacities for survival and pleasure developed through a lifetime may be dormant in an older person but can be reactivated by the creative practitioner. The social worker studies how the older person coped in the past (the resources within himself and others that he drew upon) to replicate those qualities in the present. For example, a single woman who was the caregiver of a disabled sibling and is depressed since her sibling's death may improve if she can regain some of her past role through volunteer activities. A woman with Alzheimer's disease may still retain the words to popular songs of the 20s and receive pleasure in singing them in a group in Adult Day Care. A blind and paralyzed man on a skilled nursing unit can still retain the interest and cognitive capacity to follow the world news if an FM radio is brought to his bedside.

Often, a client's strength manifests itself in difficult behavior. A nursing home resident's demanding attitude with the nurses may be his attempt to individualize a dehumanizing experience. The social worker who can identify the strength and redirect it appropriately has performed a valuable service to staff and resident.

The supervisor can remind her workers to seek out these hidden strengths by asking them to focus on what is right, rather than wrong with any given situation. What does this older person have going for him? How has he survived until now? How can you help him recognize and use his strengths to meet the current challenge?

Promoting Maximum Functioning

Older people who have sustained physical or mental losses must be helped to regain lost capacities and to resume their prior level of functioning as much as possible.

The social work practitioner does not look at one function or set of functions individually but at the gestalt. She assesses how biological, psychological, social, cultural, and organizational factors interact in the older person's performance of life sustaining and life enhancing activities. While she utilizes client strengths, she builds up environmental supports. For example, an older person who cannot climb stairs but is independent in all other ways, will be disabled if her apartment is on the third floor of a walk-up building. She will have to give up marketing, visiting, and participation in whatever activities gave her life meaning. Her functioning will improve dramatically with the move to barrier-free housing and she will no longer be disabled.

Since much of gerontological social work practice is directed toward the achievement of maximum functioning for the elder, the social work student or practitioner needs guidance in thinking about disability in a thorough, systematic manner.

It is useful to think of each disability in terms of the particular loss involved and the level of adaptation to it. The highest level of adaptation is restitution of what has been lost. This happens infrequently and usually is restricted to medical interventions, such as cataract surgery to restore vision. Compensation, or the substitution of what has been lost by a similar relationship or activity, is more common. For example, volunteer work could substitute for paid employment after retirement. Accommodation, when the older person simply lives with the loss, is the most common form of adaptation. As in the preceding example, the older person resigns herself to being homebound in the third floor apartment rather than seeking out an alternative living arrangement.

The supervisor helps the worker to access maximum functioning. Together they look at each of the older person's losses and see if the highest level of adaptation possible has been achieved. Elders who have prematurely accommodated can then be helped to better their situations. (For a fuller discussion, see Silverstone & Burack-Weiss, 1983.)

Case Example

Angela, a community social worker for Mrs. L., presented the following problem to her supervisor. Mrs. L. was currently in the hospital. She needed 24-hour care and had no space in her apartment for a live-in attendant. The discharge plan was transfer to a nursing home. Angela had tried to get the home attendant to sleep on a cot, but the agency required separate space. Her supervisor suggested a plan for two 12-hour aides. However, this turned out to be more costly. Together they then investigated short-term rehabilitation with a goal for discharge when Mrs. L. could manage on her own at night. Angela contacted the hospital worker with this plan. Mrs. L. was subsequently transferred to a nursing home that had a special rehabilitation unit.

Promoting the Least Restrictive Environment

Although the concept of least restrictive environment is essentially a legal one, it applies directly to all disciplines of gerontological practice. It means that society accepts the right of individuals to live as they wish unless they pose a threat to themselves or to others. In such situations, individual freedom is abrogated only to the extent necessary to remove the threat. The principle gives rise to many legal questions. A common example: an older woman wishes to remain in her own apartment but has grown so forgetful that she frequently leaves the gas on and wanders out alone at night. Is her behavior sufficient reason to declare incompetence and place her in a nursing home? Court appointed conservators or family members with power of attorney may call on the social worker for direction. And she, in turn, will look to her supervisor.

The notion of least restrictive environment is closely related to the idea of parsimony in medical and social interventions. One intrudes as little as possible to achieve the desired end. Thus, outpatient medical procedures are preferable to hospital admissions; home care is considered before nursing home placement.

Operationalizing the principle of least restrictive environment becomes difficult with the older person because the issues are rarely clear cut. Ascertaining risk factors and the degree of risk is subjective. Older people who are mentally competent may willingly accept the risks of living alone, risks unacceptable to families and professional service providers. Older people who are not mentally competent pose even greater dilemmas.

The worker (particularly in the community) is often faced with decisions that have no right answer, and will need the supervisor's counsel and support in thinking out the consequences of each option. This supervisory role assumes special administrative importance because of the agency's potential liability if the client is injured.

Case Example

> Evan came to supervision with Ms. S.'s eviction notice in hand. Ms. S. was a collector and had newspapers and treasures crammed into her apartment. Her landlord viewed her living environment as hazardous. Evan's supervisor explored his ideas. She discovered that Evan thought he needed to either throw everything out for her, or help her battle the landlord. As an alternative, the supervisor suggested a compromise: Ms. S. would get rid of the old newspapers and hazardous materials, but could keep the rest of her collection. The supervisor suggested that Evan contact the landlord and commit the agency to maintaining the apartment reasonably hazard free.

Promoting Ethical Practice

In gerontological social work, ethical practice dicates that elders be treated with dignity and respect. Self-determination, confidentiality, and client rights to information are but a few issues encountered on a daily basis. Unfortunately, these ideas are frequently abrogated for expediency or because the older person raises no objection. The unilateral use of elder first names, sharing medical or financial information with others without getting release, and acquiescence with relatives who plan for the elder without his participation are common occurrences.

Often the social worker assumes that because he is an ethical person, his practice is ethical as well. Or he thinks that ethical considerations are limited to life and death situations and have little bearing on his daily practice. Supervisors usually do not hear of violations of elders' rights unless a crisis results.

Because of the importance of ethical practice, the supervisor must take a proactive stand. The National Association of Social Workers (NASW) Code of Ethics, the hospital or nursing home resident's Bill of Rights, and the legislative rulings that provide fair hearings and other rights for elders are living documents that have to be made relevant to the everyday tasks of social workers. Discussions of these documents in staff meetings, case conferences, and individual supervision should be linked with practical examples to raise worker consciousness.

Treating Elders with Dignity and Respect

To avoid practice that demeans the elderly, the supervisor must demonstrate a strong ethical commitment and model ethical practice. She displays her commitment to treating the elderly with respect by conveying her beliefs and her expectations to her supervisees. She might, for example, tell a new worker about areas in which client rights are frequently breached and remind her to be alert. She should also help her think through implications of consistent ethical practice.

Case Examples

Dana agreed with her supervisor that she would treat people with dignity and respect. Dana said she would help the client resolve her fears. Her supervisor agreed but suggested that the client's son might not. He might plan to hospitalize her, stating that his mother always resisted change. Dana said she could see this was not as easy as it appeared at first. She and the supervisor agreed she would have to sit down with the client and son to discuss the options. They also discussed how she would handle the son's reactions and the additional casework it might entail.

The supervisor's own practice is also important in influencing the worker toward ethical practice:

> Mrs. K.'s daughter wanted her moved from a rehabilitation unit to a health related facility. The daughter observed how much better Mrs. K. did in an institutional setting. However, Mrs. K. refused and insisted that she wanted to go home. David's supervisor interviewed the daughter with him. In so doing, she agreed with David and the daughter that although Mrs. K. might indeed be better off in a protected setting, her own wishes were reasonable and had to be honored.

Respecting Cultural Differences

The aging population represents greater ethnic diversity than any other in the U.S. today. This factor is especially notable given the tendency for even fully assimilated Americans to return to cultural roots and mother tongues as they grow older. Attitudes toward receiving help, institutionalization, illness, and family relationships (among others) vary considerably among nationalities. The cultural component is key in every client assessment. Beyond that, cultural factors are a consideration for the client-worker relationship, and one in which the supervisor must often assume an active teaching role.

In dealing with cultural issues, the supervisor must walk a fine line. Glossing over ethnic differences in the belief that basic values and needs of all elders are essentially alike may seem the least prejudicial, most accepting approach. This method can deprive elders of their unique differences and strengths when they most need affirmation. However, emphasis on cultural characteristics of various aging populations can easily deteriorate into caricatures and stereotypes that do an even greater disservice.

However, knowledge that *some* Hispanic elders would choose Spanish food if offered as an option at the Senior Center meal program, and that *some* Black women may be denying their own health needs because they are raising young grandchildren, can be essential knowledge in the design and delivery of services to the aged.

All organizations that receive public funding are required to serve all who apply regardless of race, creed, color, or natural origin. However, the caseloads of most social agencies are not as culturally diverse as those of the aging population at large. This is because the ethnic homogeneity of the population served may, in all but metropolitan areas, be a function of the geographical catchment area of the agency. This makes it easier to amass and impart needed cultural knowledge to staff.

It is useful, in this regard, for the supervisor (or social work department) to maintain a library of readings about the cultures served for the general information of the workers. This may include fiction, poetry, and history as well as professional literature on working with special populations.

Often, worker and client are of different ethnic groups. This can create communication difficulties and practice problems.

> Suzie is a student who had emigrated from Hong Kong one year earlier. She met with Ms. P., the 60-year-old daughter of an Alzheimer's patient, to discuss placement planning. As Ms. P. told of the events leading up to her decision, she began to cry. Suzie immediately got up and left the room with an excuse that she had calls to make. When questioned by her supervisor on this unempathic response, Suzie explained that she was demonstrating respect by allowing time for Ms. P. to compose herself. The Western way of demonstrating and responding to emotions proved difficult for Suzie to accept. It was not enough to tell her that she should have remained in the room, or even to role play more feeling responses. The supervisor gave her an additional assignment, to watch and critique two popular sit-coms on television as to how emotions were handled. In this way, Suzie was not forced to give up her cultural expectations before she was ready, merely to modify them to meet professional performance expectations.

The requirements for supervisory intervention may be as great when aged clients and workers are of the same background.

Jimmy, a non-practicing Catholic student, had admitted 83-year-old Catholic Ms. D. to senior housing where weekly church services were in the Protestant faith. In reading the process recordings of their sessions, the supervisor noticed the client's longing allusions to attending mass at the church in her former neighborhood. Religious observation was not personally important to Jimmy. This perceptive student had not recognized the latent content of the communication. With the supervisor's help he was able to explore more deeply with the client. Consequently, he was able to link her up with volunteers to provide transportation to a local Catholic church.

Sometimes it is the supervisor who does not recognize problems with cultural content unless it is brought to her attention by the student.

Jane, a Protestant student from the Midwest, told the supervisor she could not understand why the primarily Jewish residents of the health care facility were continuously whining and complaining about their health. The supervisor, who was Jewish, initially became defensive. She pointed out that aging can involve multiple disabilities and, it is natural to wish to speak about them. Jane countered that she had worked with many very sick old people in her volunteer friendly visiting for the church back home. All avoided discussions of their health maintaining they were fine. The supervisor encouraged her to research different cultural attitudes toward illness. Jane's findings (that culture in which the Jewish residents were raised offered sympathy and special attention to the sick, while frontier culture valued stoicism and viewed illness as a sign of moral weakness) spurred a most informative practice conference for the whole staff.

Working Within a Systems Perspective

Social work is unique among professions in its emphasis on improving the interaction between individuals and the environments in which they live. The elder is composed of multiple systems (physical, psychological, social), and his environment is constituted of systems (family, friends, neighbors, and helping organizations). Because the older person is often frail and dependent on the environment for support, the gerontological social worker will probably spend at least half her time conferring with client collaterals and other helping professionals. This holds true for community and institutional practice settings. Consequently, it is not enough for the social worker to be proficient in enabling encounters with the elder. She must also be able to mediate with him and advocate for him within the larger system.

Because social work education often does not devote much attention to teaching these skills, often the task falls to the supervisor. Sometimes counselling is required. At other times, systems work is all that is needed. Gerontological social work is a blend of both types of service. Supervisors must legitimatize both types of intervention in teaching and in evaluation of worker performance.

Case Example:

> Her supervisor noted that Pat, a bright, sensitive worker with excellent casework and group work skills, was frustrated with bureaucratic issues. She viewed these problems as obstacles to real work. She became angry with hospital nurses who interrupted her. Her supervisor began to discuss system intervention not as a problem, but as a concept. Pat read and responded to some selected readings and a discussion of practice principles. She began to understand how to work within a larger system.

Setting Appropriate Goals

One often hears of the importance of setting limited goals for the elderly, as if clients of all ages were not limited in some way by their personalities or environment. It is more useful to think of goals for the elderly as being appropriate to the circumstances and wishes of the client. Gerontological social workers seek to maintain a current level of functioning or adaptation to a lower level of functioning more often than radical change or growth. However, there are opportunities for elder improvement and worker gratification.

Small interventions can be productive with the elderly. The trusting relationship with a friendly visitor, transportation to a senior center, a meals on wheels program, or a visit to the beauty parlor may add to the quality of life.

Gerontological social work practice promotes life enhancing and life sustaining interventions. No one gets up in the morning only to dress, wash, or perform any of the other "activities of daily living" with which service providers are often preoccupied. While we must perform these tasks, they are a means to an end, not an end in themselves. Social workers must seek and promote those individualized sources of pleasure that give the older person reason to survive.

Conclusion

Chapter 2

Stages of Helping, Learning, and Teaching

Adult educators use the term "teachable moment" to refer to the optimum time for the learner to absorb and use new knowledge. We have all had the experience of being able to apply a professional maxim for the first time. Something "clicks" and we know that the insight is now a part of us. We have discovered the relevance of the knowledge. We need it. We can apply it. It works.

The "teachable moment," then, is the time when what you teach can be immediately applied to what the student or practitioner needs to know. The timing, setting, and content should approximate as much as possible the normative learning needs of the worker.

Fortunately, there *is* a predictable sequence to the learning needs of gerontological social workers. Each worker's personality and experience may influence the timing and expression of needs but not its essential character. Gerontological social workers, like their elderly clients, are confronting an existential issue — how to deal with the losses endemic to the last stage of the life span. In so doing, they experience in supervision many of the same emotional reactions to loss that their aged clients have.

The supervisor's understanding of these responses helps with elderly clients and beginning practitioners in the field of aging. Practice approaches with the older person at each stage of adaptation find their parallel in teaching approaches that help the worker.

THE LOSSES OF LATE LIFE

Loss, the deprivation of or being without what one has had and valued, occurs throughout the life span, but accelerates in the later years. While there is wide individual variation in chronology, the onset of losses typically occurs in the sixth decade and increases thereafter.

Retirement, potentially traumatic in itself, can foster accompanying losses: reduction of income and status, and diminished opportunities for socialization and self-actualization. The incidence of widowhood increases. Significant others lost through death or relocation are less likely to be replaced by new relationships.

As time goes on, losses of external resources are increasingly accompanied by losses of the self, such as sensory, cognitive, and functional impairments and chronic health problems associated with the aging process. Consequently, the older person becomes dependent on others to a greater extent than at other adult stages of the life span.

THE MEANING OF LOSSES TO ELDER AND WORKER

The following discussion is based on four premises:

1. Adaptation to losses of self and significant others is a primary developmental task of the aged client. The gerontological practitioner must learn how to handle this process.
2. Each worker's experience with loss parallels that of the client.
3. These responses to loss give rise to attitudes and behaviors in the client-worker relationship and the worker-supervisor relationship.
4. As the worker helps the aged client adapt to losses, so does the supervisor help the worker adapt to the losses suffered by aged clients.

Contemporary theorists agree that individuals experience a pattern of emotional responses on the journey from loss to adaptation. Not everyone shows all responses and using a sequential process may oversimplify the case. However, the schema is useful in depicting common experiences of elders and workers.

We identify five distinct states commonly exhibited in response to late life losses (shock/disbelief, denial, bargaining, anger/depression, acceptance). Then we discuss the ways in which these states are manifested in both elder and worker and suggest supervisory strategies to assist elders and workers in satisfactory resolution.

SHOCK AND DISBELIEF

The Elder

Aging is a continuous process, and old age is an anticipated status. Nevertheless, the dawning of awareness is an individual and shocking occurrence often occasioned by a specific event: a medical diagnosis, the funeral of a contemporary, the chance remark of a stranger. And it hits, "I am now old." At first, these are fleeting moments soon dwarfed by other experiences, but as the moments accumulate the reality is ever-present.

There is disbelief in the changing body so at odds with the inner self, shock at the often insidious lack of respect accorded older people in our culture, and surprise at the paucity of help available in times of need. For example, many older people anticipate that health and home care services will be covered by Medicare, but discover that many expenses will have to come from retirement income.

The individual for whom the reality of old age has just set in needs time to reckon with his feelings and his options. What experiences can be harnessed to meet present day demands? What new activities or interests can offer gratification? Of course, this sorting process does not customarily take place on a conscious level. Most often, it can be inferred by observation of the elder's trial and error efforts at mastery.

What strategies work with the elder in shock and disbelief? The social worker can primarily be helpful by offering concrete assistance and information which the client needs to understand his changed situation. Supportive counselling, focussed on identification of client strengths and resources, is the intervention of choice. Premature focus on dysfunctional aspects of the client's life situation diminishes the ego when it most needs reinforcement. In fact, support and concrete assistance may be all that is needed to enhance the client's natural processes of adaptation to an altered life situation.

The Social Worker

The social worker who enters gerontological social work practice also encounters an initial period of shock and disbelief. Myths and stereotypes about aging are debunked one by one leaving uncertainty and ambiguity in their wake.

There is also justifiable shock at the lack of congruence between the needs of elderly clients and the service system (of which one's own agency is a part) designed to meet them. A process of sorting out occurs as the social worker new to gerontology struggles to overcome erroneous beliefs and assimilate new learning. Not all old people are like the worker's grandparents. Older people have sexual feelings and may express them with the worker. In addition, their middle-aged children may ask for the worker's help in making Solomon-like decisions about their parents' welfare.

The student or worker who anticipated that gerontological social work would involve friendly visiting and concrete services to appreciative older people is surprised by the hostility and pathology that is as present in this client population as any other. The worker wonders: Is this the field for me? What of my past beliefs are still relevant? What must be changed?

As the worker's sense of security is challenged, she often searches for something to hold on to, such as concrete information about entitlements, agency policies and procedures. Students are usually full of "what ifs." They expect a formula response that will work for all elders. This period of worker self-consciousness is not to be confused with self-awareness. The worker is not so much in touch with her feelings as at their mercy. The worker's struggle for control of her reactions may thus usurp her concentration on the specific client and problem.

The supervisor's task in this initial phase is to respond to the worker's disequilibrium by answering only what the worker asks to know. This is not the time to point out all the complexities that lurk beneath the surface of the case which may serve to overwhelm the worker even further. The supervisor does well to center on the worker's observation of clients — how clearly does she see and report what is going on? The goal here is to alleviate uncertainty by focussing worker attention on what she can do, even at this stage of inexperience. For the same reason, the supervisor should not analyze the worker's interactions with clients or suggest exercises to increase self-awareness at this time. Such evaluations increase self-consciousness and a sense of inadequacy when the worker is struggling for mastery.

As supportive counseling is most effective with the older person in the period of shock and disbelief, so supportive supervision is the approach of choice with the new worker. The goal in both cases is non-interference in the individual's natural processes of adaptation and ultimately the mastery of new circumstances.

DENIAL

The Elder

Every seasoned practitioner has stories about the aged client who doesn't want to be with "those old people." In fact, congregate services in the community and in institutions are often spurned for that reason. Denial also appears in more subtle guises, such as non-compliance with a medical regime, refusal of necessary services, habitual interactions with others that are no longer appropriate.

Of course, denial can be functional in old age. Refusal to acknowledge a loss may actually contribute to successful adaptation in situations where nothing can or must be done. It is only when denial interferes with needed care that it must be challenged.

What do we do with the older person locked in dysfunctional denial? The worker should support the elder's positive coping attempts. Then the worker should explain the reality without euphemism or jargon: "You are trying hard to handle a difficult situation. This is what you are facing. This is what could happen to you. I am here to help you." The client may first respond with anger or even greater denial. However, the mere statement of the reality helps the client begin to consider alternative ways of handling his situation.

The Social Worker

The social worker new to gerontology will often exhibit denial. She may take one of two polar approaches to clients: the aged are like everyone else, only older; the aged are a special case for which no prior knowledge applies. As a result of her own shock and disbelief and struggle to apply her knowledge and skill, she may become too generic or specific in her approach.

The worker who resolves that the aged are like everyone else will gloss over cohort, sensory, or cognitive differences to make her cases fit into practice models she has learned at school or with other populations. Her emphasis on contracting, problem definition, and mutual goal setting will be met blankly by many of the elderly.

At the other extreme is the worker who resolves that the aged are a special case for whom a professional approach is irrelevant. She may enter into an ambiguous social relationship with the client or act as a surrogate child, promoting confusion in the client and worker relationship.

The task of the supervisor is to help the worker discover what general knowledge base is applicable and what must be altered in work with the aged. For example, the contract with a confused elder may be simply that the worker is a person from an agency that helps old people and will visit at regular intervals to see how he is getting along. This contract may need repeating at each meeting and cannot be eliminated without blurring professional and personal roles. Such ambiguity could prove ultimately destructive to the helping relationship.

As the denial of the older person is best addressed by a clear statement and re-enforcement of reality supported by a caring worker, so is the denial of the worker most profitably challenged by didactic teaching and assigned readings by a caring supervisor. The worker may now realize that her all-or-nothing approach is not working. However, she may be hard pressed to say why. Psychodynamic understanding of the aging personality, theories of aging, and other conceptual approaches are best introduced at this time.

BARGAINING

The Elder

The recognition of loss and attendant painful feelings is usually gradual and intermittent. As loss enters the older person's consciousness, a period of bargaining may ensue. Thus, the older person will accept the transportation and escort to medical appointments but not the homemaker, the high intensity lamp to improve vision but not the cane outdoors that would identify her as blind.

Struggle for control is at the heart of the bargaining stage. The awareness of what is irrevocably gone is sinking in, and the older person is testing the limits of his autonomy and power. Behind this often lies an unexpressed wish for the impossible, and a bit of magical thinking—if I only get back to my own home, all will be as it was before.

Anticipation and preparation for threatening new experiences helps the elder imaginatively ready himself for what is to come. This is also a good time for encouraging reminiscence and mourning of past periods of better functioning. Interpretation of the present behavior as an effort to hold on to what is no more follows naturally from reminiscence. It may precede acceptance of a changed self.

The Social Worker

For the social worker, the bargaining phase can most often be deduced from attitude and behavior. The worker will be preoccupied with one case above all others in the caseload, or over-identify with the older person in family interactions.

As with the older person in the bargaining stage, the issue is one of control. However, there is a slight difference: if I just do enough for this client she will be able to . . . or not have to . . .

The supervisory task is to help the worker identify the unrecognized wish behind her over-activity and accept the limits of her power. For the worker, as with the older person, confronting her lack of control over the ultimate outcome of the situation is painful. The existence of circumstances beyond one's influence and the limits of help giving and help receiving are hard to acknowledge. At this time, the worker may be most responsive to experiential supervisory techniques that foster self-awareness.

Workers may be embarrassed when confronted with their grandiose thoughts. However, they usually are thankful for an opportunity for discussion. Workers who care the most are usually the most severely afflicted and supervisors should validate their investment in client well-being before challenging over-zealous behavior.

ANGER AND DEPRESSION

Anger and depression are closely linked emotions in old age. They share the same root: feelings of helplessness and hopelessness. At times they coexist, with one masquerading as the other. They are the most common responses of clients and workers to loss.

Anger

The Elder

The anger the older person feels when confronted with losses may be manifested in attitudes and behaviors consonant with the individual's previous life style and personality pattern, reflecting a sense of helplessness.

The more assertive elder will direct and express anger toward the nearest targets: family, other caregivers, and, often, the social worker. Dissatisfaction with services, and criticism of her helping efforts cut deep with the worker who is trying so hard yet can never please. Client anger may also be expressed passively, such as forgetting appointments or failing to follow through on agreed-upon tasks.

The novice worker often responds defensively to outbursts, pointing out the falsity and reality of each assertion or trying to quiet the client with reassurance. Such interventions lead to client-worker power struggles and a breakdown of the alliance.

First, the worker must identify the source of the elder's anger. She must accept what is appropriately directed to her and adjust her practice accordingly. She must not personalize that which arises from the client's own feelings of loss. Finally, she must allow a safe place and sufficient time for the client to express negative feelings not easily tolerated by family and friends.

For the client who expresses anger passively, a gentle confrontation, with care to support the ego, is often in order. Pointing out the disparity between what is said and what is done invites the client to express negative feelings directly.

The Social Worker

The worker at this stage best receives help in handling client anger through recognizing and coping with the resonating anger in herself. When worker's anger is justifiably directed toward an unresponsive service system, the supervisor should teach skills in working with the environment; advocacy, brokering and mediating with one's own and other systems. With students, this is a good time to introduce required process recordings of formal and informal interventions with staff and other agency personnel.

When the worker personalizes the older person's anger, the supervisor must help her maintain focus on the client assessment. Understanding the possible origin of the behavior is the first step toward helping the worker help the client ventilate and then direct appropriately. Or, in the more difficult case, the worker may need assistance in identifying and accepting her own dysfunctional interactive patterns with the client that have spawned the anger.

Sometimes, of course, the worker's anger at agency, supervisor, or the entire service system may not be a reflection of client responses at all, but may arise out of her own deep dissatisfaction at receiving too much interference, or too little support, or perceived lack of progress with clients, or personal problems unrelated to the professional role.

As the worker's task is to move the angry elder from reactive expressions of anger to proactive means of control, so the supervisor must move the worker from reactive anger at the system to proactive advocacy efforts on the elder's and his own behalf.

Depression

The Elder

As anger is characterized by helplessness, depression is marked by hopelessness or a sense of futility. Elders suffering a clinical depression will, of course, experience a variety of additional symptoms requiring a range of interdisciplinary professional interventions. However, for the majority of older clients, depression is more difficult to diagnose, often veiled by psychosomatic complaints or paradoxical reactions. Withdrawal of interest in activities may be incorrectly interpreted as being age-syntonic. Agitation may be handled as disruptive behavior rather than linked to an underlying mood disturbance. Or depression may signal the early stages of dementia. The depressed elder views his situation as "all or nothing." If he cannot be restored to who he was before, what is the use?

The elder's sense of dependency and helplessness mirrors that of his early life. Now, as then, he must borrow strength from the bond with a caring, supportive figure. This role is appropriately filled by the social worker.

Within the supportive relationship there are many useful approaches. The most immediate is the process of partializing and prioritizing, breaking the situation into manageable units. Then, the elder can decide which to tackle first.

The Social Worker

As the older person may become hopeless and despairing in the face of irreplaceable losses, the worker often suffers a similar paralysis of thought and action when confronted with the multiple losses and poor prognosis of many elderly clients. How can the worker provide hope when she has none?

The supervisor can be most helpful here in sharing her own professional experiences. For example, a wheelchair-bound woman on the skilled nursing unit will remain in that state regardless of fine social work intervention. However, the mobilization of her inner and outer resources can lead to improved psycho-social functioning and life satisfaction for her. Selective sharing of the supervisor's own positive experiences and best-case scenarios can help the worker imagine the possible and the hopeful.

As the elder must adjust self-expectations to meet the reality of her losses, so the worker needs to grasp the concept that work with the aged often involves maintenance of existing strengths rather than dramatic improvements. In fact, incremental, changes may be all that are achieved.

The supervisor who can find satisfaction in the incremental growth of the worker demonstrates this attitude through role modelling.

ACCEPTANCE

The Elder

Acceptance of loss is considered in all theories to be the culmination of the adaptive process. This may not be the case with the aged. Acceptance of loss is often marked by premature accommodation to situations that could yet be improved. Families and physicians often contribute to this attitude through global attribution of late-life problems to old age, rather than to a remediable cause.

The elder who openly acknowledges all his losses and calmly attributes them to his age may be seen by the inexperienced worker as philosophical if not realistic. She is relieved of responsibility. If the client is not troubled, why should she be? Often she may focus on the specific request for help, bypassing the broad-based assessment that would reveal if the client were indeed functioning at the optimum level possible given his disabilities. Sensory, cognitive, and mobility deficits are often correctable at least in part by introduction of aids, training, and minor changes in life style. All of these factors must be explored before concluding that the elder has satisfactorily adapted to loss.

However, if current functioning *is* the best possible, it is the time to introduce life-enhancing activities. It is the time for mutual investigation of new activities or interests to replace those that are irretrievably lost. The worker can contribute her knowledge of community programs and opportunities.

Sometimes the client reaches acceptance after a long period of worker investment. The relationship is so solid and gratifying on both sides that it is difficult for the worker to terminate. The worker's task here is to review with the client their work together to date and to establish if there are future goals to be met. Even if optimum functioning has been reached and there is no immediate need for ongoing contact, new problematic circumstances may arise which the worker stands ready to move in on. A period of less frequent contact is a useful prelude to termination allowing the client a chance to act more independently while still assured of the worker's involvement.

The Social Worker

The supervisor whose worker has accepted the losses of her elderly clients faces the same range of reactions. She is relieved that she can now move on to more problematic workers, takes pride in her job well done, vacillates between holding on and letting go, and sometimes relies on the worker's report that all is well.

As with the client, mutual review and appraisal of work to date vis-à-vis performance expectations of agency or school is in order. If criteria have not been met, a specific plan with a time frame for accomplishment should be set in place. If criteria have been met, next steps include a renegotiation of the supervisory contract to allow for increased worker autonomy, always with the opportunity for consultation and support. Worker gains can be consolidated by placing her in an advisory, and in time supervisory, capacity with newer workers. This role forces her to conceptualize and teach her practice.

In summary, the social worker and practitioner are more alike than different, joined in the very human struggle of adaptation to loss. Understanding the parallel process and making use of the "teachable moment" can enhance supervisory effectiveness with workers and workers' effectiveness with elders.

Chapter 3

Styles of Helping, Learning, and Teaching

STYLES OF HELPING

Elderly clients and their social workers are alike in that each has his own characteristic style of approaching new situations and assimilating new information. Elderly clients and their social workers are also alike in that they are frequently dependent on others to accomplish their aims. As the clients look to the worker for help, so the worker looks to the supervisor.

The supervisor is constantly presented with situations that require action. Clients, families, agencies, or communities expect a result, action, solution, or resolution. With the student social worker, it is achievement of semester field performance criteria. With the social worker, it is meeting agency demands for productivity and accountability.

So there are many pressures on supervisor and worker to *Do For*. It is, after all, a quick fix. The supervisor tells the worker what to do. The worker tells the older person what to do, or bypasses the older person completely and does the task herself. Although most doing for is not ultimately effective, it feels good at the time to have the answers. Doing for relieves the feelings of helplessness and anxiety.

Almost as satisfying is *Not Doing*. Sometimes not doing is a first response to the elder's or worker's request for help. More often it is a reaction to the failure of doing: "I've carried the ball long enough," we say, "Now it's your turn." For the older person it may be rationalized as "Self-Determination." For the worker,

27

"Accepting responsibility for his own learning." Either way, it lets everyone off the hook for awhile.

Doing With, a sharing of the responsibility, is thought of as desirable. However, shared tasks pose problems of their own. Who does what? When? How?

Actually, *Doing For, Not Doing*, or *Doing With* may all be appropriate methods of serving the elderly and of supervising workers. But the choice of the strategy should not be propelled by internal needs or external pressures. What is needed is an assessment of dependency in each situation, and the method of doing the work that best meets each need.

Assessing the Situation

Assessment of the specific older person or specific worker in terms of their need and capacity for doing is based on a few general assumptions about the nature of dependence.

1. *Dependence is partial, not total.* However disabled, the older person can do something—even if it is just to raise a finger to indicate yes or no. However inexperienced, the worker can do something—perhaps she can engage but not contract, handle concrete matters but not emotional content.

2. *Dependence is temporary, not permanent.* The older person's disability curve is not a straight dive downhill anymore than the worker's learning curve is a straight upward climb. There are many plateaus, unexpected spurts forward, disheartening regressions.

3. *Dependence may be in doing, not planning.* There is the apocryphal story of the old woman who said, "just because I need help crossing the street doesn't mean I don't know where I am going." Or the worker who understands the purpose of a family conference and can set it up very well; she just doesn't know what to do with all the people once they get there.

4. *Dependence may be in planning, not doing.* If the older person is asked, "do you want a homemaker?" and says, "no," that is not self-determination. Older people may lack the information or the opportunity to talk through alternatives that are necessary for informed decision making. The worker may be able to follow through on directions, but unable to initiate a plan.

In short, we cannot speak globally of dependence or discuss in general terms whether it is better to do or not to do. Rather, our assessments of the individual elder or worker situation must specify: dependent in planning or action? dependent for how long? dependent in what ways?

Doing With

Doing With ensures optimum functioning of the elder and the worker. This method fosters control and mastery over what can be done alone and supports what needs the help of another.

Doing With operationalizes the concepts of mutuality and reciprocity in the social work process.

Doing With is sharing the work. And each piece of work has many many tasks. Qualifying for Medicaid can pose a dozen or more tasks for the elder; relating to the decision making and assembling the documents required for eligibility. The elder will be able to complete some tasks alone. With others, he will require the worker's assistance.

Similarly, acquiring the skills to see the elder through the Medicaid application encompasses many tasks for the worker. Some of these can best be mastered through didactic teaching, some through reading, some only through experience. Sometimes a task may not be assigned to one or another but be handled by worker and supervisor, or worker and elder. When the worker accompanies the client to the Medicaid interview he is offering support as well as role modelling ways of handling anxiety-provoking situations. When the supervisor asks the worker how she will prepare the elder for the Medicaid interview and help her consider the pros and cons of various approaches, she is modelling how one tries to anticipate the consequences of various alternatives.

Doing For

What of the unilateral *Doing For* that workers and supervisors continually find themselves pulled into? Is it ever appropriate by itself?

Doing For may well be the important first intervention with the elder when physical or mental impairment renders him incapable of a task and there are no friends or relatives to act on his behalf, or when technical agency communication is required. It is also a good point of entry with the suspicious elder who requires tangible proof of the worker's investment before he can trust. The hands-on intervention of the worker can provide the nurturing environment in which the chronically dependent elder can function optimally, as well as legitimize the dependency needs of the staunchly self-reliant older person.

Doing For may well be the first intervention for the beginning worker who requires a grounding in information and skills before she can meet her clients with any confidence. *Doing For* is the entitlement of any worker when the demands of the assignment exceed her capacities or when she needs the support of a caring supervisor. *Doing For* needs no apology when used appropriately. It is only destructive when it preempts the elder or worker's own ideas and abilities to meet challenges of the situation.

In summary, dependence and independence are two sides of the same coin. We negotiate them as workers, as supervisors, and as people every day of our personal and professional lives.

STYLES OF LEARNING

Many social work educators have attempted to identify learning types and styles. All agree that it is rare to find anyone exhibiting a pure type. More likely, individuals are prone to one form of learning and use the others to a lesser degree.

What is the value of this information to a gerontological social work supervisor? Understanding of her own predominant style of learning and that of her supervisees can point the way to more productive teaching strategies.

What are the types of learners and how can they be identified? What are the types of teaching and how can they best be applied to each type of learner?

The following two sections build upon various models found in the literature. The first summarizes and illustrates three predominant types of learners. The second summarizes and illustrates three predominant teaching strategies of use in supervision.

Types of Learners

There are three basic types of learners: the intuitive learner, the intellectual learner, and the practical learner. Each is identified by her dominant mode of response to a situation.

Let us imagine that Mrs. W. reports that severe arthritic pain kept her from attending her great grandson's first birthday party. The intuitive learner would most likely respond with how difficult it must have been to miss the event. The intellectual learner would be more apt to ask specific questions about the symptoms and medical treatment. The practical learner would probably move quickly into a discussion of adaptive equipment and transportation that could facilitate participation in such activities.

Obviously, any or all of the above responses could be appropriate given the assessment of Mrs. W. and her situation. It is the frequency of one kind of response, regardless of the circumstances, that identifies the dominant mode of learning.

The Intuitive Learner

The Intuitive Learner leads with her senses. She is empathic with the emotions of her elderly clients. Empathy, in this sense, is clearly separate from altruism. Most practitioners with the aged are motivated by their *feeling for* the client and desire to be helpful. The Intuitive Learner goes one step beyond; she *feels with* the client.

This situation can have positive and negative consequences. Because she is so attuned to the feelings of others, this worker says what others wish to hear. She engages a wide range of clients easily. She generally has a good ear for the latent content of client communications, although her empathy will sometimes lead her to accept all client productions at face value. She is more often accepting than judgmental of the various maladaptive ways many elders choose to live their lives. She is particularly able with the sensorially or cognitively impaired and is often creative in her assessments and interventions.

Judy, a middle-aged woman who entered social work school after working many years as a free-lance artist, performed two stunning interventions in her first week in her first placement. She had never set foot in a nursing home before and had not read anything about the aged. Mr. B., an 87-year-old man with advanced Alzheimer's Disease had been admitted three days earlier. Floor staff could not handle his agitation. She sat with him a bit and recognized that the focus of his distress centered upon three abstract paintings hanging on the walls. Hearing from the family of his prior interest in horse racing, she removed the pictures and replaced them with magazine illustrations of equestrian pastimes. He quieted almost immediately. Down the hall was Mrs. P., a 72-year-old woman, who was aphasic following a stroke. Her only method of communication was guttural cries and moans. Within an hour Judy could differentiate between and respond to sounds of sorrow, rage, and pleasure.

The Intuitive Learner will take risks, not all of which have successful outcomes. But her genuine feeling for the client usually sees her through the worst blunders.

Sometimes the Intuitive Learner may so join with the client that she is unable to visualize, much less express, a differing point of view. When the elder says she will not accept a homemaker because she fears theft, she takes on the client's fear. When the elder is angry with his son, she too becomes angry.

Another hallmark of the Intuitive Learner is that she is frequently in "over her head" and does not recognize it. Because she is so comfortable exploring feelings, she may inadvertently open up issues with the client that she does not know how to handle. In an extreme case, she may so emphatize with a suicidal elder she cannot imagine an alternative reality.

The supervisor of an Intuitive Learner will need to help her make conscious what is now done naturally. As the supervisor labels techniques, and builds in the theoretical underpinnings of practice, the learner can identify and so control her responses. Then, she will be able to plan their use appropriately.

The Intellectual Learner

As the Intuitive Learner leads with her senses, the Intellectual Learner leads with her mind. She wants to anticipate, to prepare for encounters with elders. She believes that the more she knows beforehand, the better the result.

She is often strong in observational and analytic skills, but may be slow to put these into practice. She is more comfortable exploring facts than feelings. Her interviews with clients tend toward a question and answer format.

Often she is particularly interested in organizational structure and issues. When interested in clinical work, the Intellectual Learner is drawn to theoretical approaches and practice models. She welcomes lists of readings. She delights in discussion of personality dynamics and manifestations she may see in her own caseload.

Her risks are calculated and most often work out well because of advance planning.

Avery was assigned ten cases her first week of employment at the Home Care agency. Her first task was to make contact with each of the clients and their homemakers. A week later she had not had one contact, and her supervisor thought that hiring her had been a poor decision. However, in the conference it turned out that Avery had used the time to read every piece of literature about the agency, the services offered, the referral sources and procedures, and the client records. She had also discussed the cases with other members of the interdisciplinary staff. For each elder and homemaker she had drawn up a list of possible issues and responses. Feeling in control, she was able to move into the work quickly in the second week.

The Intellectual Learner may pose a challenge to an Intuitive supervisor, as in the following situation encountered by one of the authors.

The supervisor told Lois that the client just assigned was unpredictable; perhaps she would wish to speak, perhaps she would not. She suggested that Lois "play it by ear." Lois exploded with a scathingly accurate imitation of the supervisor's attitude and tone, ending poignantly, *"I* can't do that. *I* have to know." It was a moment of revelation for the supervisor. Not every supervisee could be—or should be—an imitation of her. Clearly, a different teaching approach was needed for this type of learner.

The supervisor of the Intellectual Learner will need to help her gain awareness of how her feelings affect her work with clients. As she is better able to integrate intellectual and emotional ways of understanding, she will gain ease in dealing with emotionally-charged material and ambiguous situations.

The Practical Learner

If we continue with the analogy of leading with the senses and the mind, the Practical Learner leads with her hands. She is guided by a desire to make things better and seeks every opportunity to perform a concrete service. Because the elderly present many concrete service needs, she is particularly useful in work with this population. In every agency, she is the one with up-to-date procedural information and good contacts in entitlement agencies.

The Practical Learner is less attuned to problems of clients for which there is no immediate solution. Unlike the Intuitive Learner who feels the pain as her own or the Intellectual Learner who tries to understand where the pain comes from, the Practical Learner might not recognize the pain at all.

Because she approaches life in a pragmatic fashion, she may expect the same from elders and families. She may become puzzled or angry when they do not act in their own best interests.

Priscilla told Mr. J.'s son exactly the documentation he would need to apply for Medicaid for his father and coached him on every step in the process. When she called to check on the application, she was shocked to learn that he had not even made an appointment. Although he had expressed remorse about being unable to support his father, she could not take in the emotional impact of this information and its probable effect on his behavior.

The Practical Learner, like the Intellectual Learner, explores facts with greater facility than feelings. However, while the Intellectual Learner's goal is understanding the problem better, the Practical Learner's goal is uncovering a solution. In her desire to bring about change quickly, she tends to take over more of the work of a case than she needs to. If she is unable to provide a solution, she is usually ready with advice and suggestions to the client on how he can manage his problems. His lack of follow-through is a source of frustration to her.

The Practical Learner learns primarily from trial and error. Over time, she realizes that some interventions are usually effective and so broadens their application to different cases. She recognizes that other interventions do not work and gradually stops using them.

The particular challenge of supervising a Practical Learner lies in appreciating and supporting the very real skills required to carry out concrete tasks, while demanding a deeper level of practice. The worker needs to become more reflective about the meanings and consequences of her behavior and that of her clients. With increased theoretical understanding and self-awareness, she will be better able to enable clients to think through solutions and consequences of decisions, and to act on their own behalf.

In her second year of placement, Lisa was still rushing to action before fully exploring the elder's problem. Her supervisor asked that she go through a day of interviews without once making a suggestion or offering to do something herself. Instead, the supervisor suggested that she "just listen" and respond if necessary with rephrasing or empathic comments. Lisa reported the day was "excruciating." She kept holding back and feeling powerless. However, she did realize that the elders accepted her even when she did not do something. And that was a lesson that stayed with her.

Again, it is rare to find a worker who fits only one of the above categories. However, identifying the learner's primary style can help the supervisor and the learner to decide what emphasis to place on the following teaching strategies.

STYLES OF TEACHING

There are three major types of teaching that are utilized within the supervisory relationship: collaborative discussion, didactic instruction, and experiential exercises. Each method has its virtues. Each method complements the others. The proportion of any one type of teaching depends upon the type of learner and the issue to be taught.

Collaborative Discussion

Collaborative Discussion is the mutual give and take of conversational discourse. It is the most frequently used teaching technique. In educational supervision, it is initiated by the supervisor to explore the student's thinking on a case. In administrative supervision and consultation, it is often initiated by the worker who has identified the problem for discussion.

Collaborative Discussion can be useful in modelling the way to approach a problem through logical analysis. As the worker gets used to conferring with the supervisor, he will be more likely to analyze it on his own.

The supervisor should ask rather than assume why a particular intervention or idea governed the worker. Sometimes good intentions underlie an insensitive response or ineffective action. A student or beginning worker may need support for a good intention before being able to accept criticism for an intervention.

> Sally had asked a depressed man if he would take a whole bottle of pills if he had them. The supervisor was appalled but restrained herself and asked Sally what she had been thinking at this moment. Sally said that she had read that suicidal ideation should be explored with depressed people, and this was the only way she could think of to do it.

Collaborative Discussion can be enriched by the use of analogy. Drawing analogies between the learner's own life and difficulties in practice can promote greater understanding.

Jeff complained that he did not see why residents of the skilled nursing unit were so cliquish and gossipy. They were all old and sick, why couldn't they get along together? The supervisor pointed out that congregate living had certain similarities, whether it was in a college dormitory or in a nursing home. Were there any people in Jeff's dormitory he would not want to be seen with? Did his group of friends go out of their way to invite others to join them?

Collaborative Discussion also benefits from the skills of generalizing and partializing. Generalizing takes place in two ways. It is a way in which the supervisor organizes elder attitudes or behaviors into a pattern. In so doing, she helps the student or worker make links between theory and practice.

Mrs. K. tells you that she cannot sleep and thinks constantly about things she should have done. These may be symptoms of a clinical depression. Let's look at whether she fills some of the other criteria of a clinical depression before deciding what to do next.

Generalizing also allows the supervisor to apply the worker's experience to professional situations.

Mr. J. refused to speak to you the first times you called; but your persistence paid off and now he seeks your help. This is frequently the case with protective service clients. Can you think of other situations in your caseload that could benefit from this approach?

Partializing is another useful technique of collaborative discussion. It involves breaking a problem into manageable parts.

Let's list the problems the K sisters have had since the death of their caregiving niece. They are mourning her loss, unable to manage household chores or finances. The landlord is threatening eviction. The nephew is advocating for nursing home placement. What is the most urgent need? What is most amenable to the interventions of our agency?

In Collaborative Discussion, it is wise to begin discussion in a manner that accents strengths and mitigates deficits of learning style before looking at the case at hand.

Let us imagine supervision on the case of Miss G., an 87-year-old community resident for whom a nursing home is being discussed. We will envision how the Collaborative Discussion might evolve with the three types of learners previously identified.

Ally, an intuitive learner, laments that Miss G. will surely die if she has to go into a nursing home. The supervisor recognizes that Ally is expressing her own feelings about placement, over-identifying with Miss G. Ally needs help separating her thoughts and feelings from those of her clients. The supervisor helps Ally look at differences between her life experiences, current situation, and personality and that of Miss G. before they begin to discuss Miss G.'s plan.

John, an intellectual learner, announces that Miss G. will not survive long in the nursing home. The supervisor knows that John has read about the high mortality rate in the first few months after nursing home admission. He needs help integrating this information with the case at hand. She points out that studies have shown that the highest risk is posed to those who are most ill on admission. Adequate preparation and involvement of the elder in the planning minimizes the risks. She also shares a few clinical experiences of her own of nursing home admissions. She is careful to include her emotional reactions to the placement. In this way, she urges him to consider his feelings and those of Miss G. Then, they discuss how he might work with her on the move.

Amy, a pragmatic learner, comes into supervision and says she is ready to take on a new case since her client, Miss G., is all set to enter the nursing home. Because Amy takes pride in her ability to maintain frail elders in the community, she has interpreted the placement as a professional failure. She has "written off" Miss G., unaware of the emotional support she can offer in the transition period. The supervisor helps Amy review her work with Miss G., pointing out what she has done and the circumstances that were beyond her control. They discuss how Miss G.'s daily routine will be different in the nursing home, and how Amy can prepare her for the changes.

Collaborative Discussion benefits all learners to a certain degree. It forms a useful bridge between the supervisor's didactic instruction and the worker's experiential exercises. It also models how the worker most effectively can interact with clients. However, collaborative discussion easily digresses unless the supervisor maintains control and focus.

Didactic Teaching

Didactic Teaching consists of straight information giving. The supervisor gives assigned readings or oral presentations relating to basic knowledge skills, and tasks to be done in each case.

Didactic Teaching is what one typically associates with the teaching role, familiar to both supervisor and worker from their years in the educational system. Because it is very comfortable, many supervisors use it exclusively. It feels good to be the impartor of wisdom. Most workers feel that they are indeed "getting something" when they emerge from a session with a notepad full of instructions. However, used exclusively, it blocks off the worker's participation in and responsibility for her own learning.

Paradoxically, it is the Intellectual Learner, the one who likes didactic instruction the most, who benefits the least. She will revel in the information and theories that are given (and inflate the ego of the supervisor by respect for all she knows). She may have difficulty translating knowledge into practice. Week after week, she experiences the same problems in her cases. Understanding does not inexorably lead to doing.

For the Intellectual Learner, Didactic Teaching is best followed by experiential exercises. This is a necessary prelude to deciding what to do next on that case. The Practical Learner also expects and takes well to Didactic Teaching if it is informational. Theoretical or personality dynamics explanations are best illustrated with case examples. The Intuitive Learner can benefit most from Didactic Teaching. It is illuminating for her to get an outside perspective on her feelings — to recognize that there is a body of knowledge and skills that validates her impressions and provides a structured way to offer help.

Experiential Teaching

Experiential Exercises are a form of re-entering past or anticipating future interactions between worker and client to work out interventive strategies. Role Play and Line by Line reading of recording are two methods of this approach. While Line by Line can be used effectively with workers, it depends upon the presence of detailed process recording that usually is done only by students.

Experiential Exercises are initially used by supervisors and workers with some reluctance. However, their usefulness becomes readily apparent once the initial embarrassment is overcome.

Role Play

Role Play can be done with the supervisor playing the worker and the worker playing the client, or the other way around.

When the supervisor plays the worker she does more than model good responses or provide the words the worker may be lacking. She listens carefully to the way the worker portrays his client and for client feelings that have not emerged in the worker's recordings or oral presentations.

> Lisa played Mrs. W. with an exaggerated whining tone. It was immediately evident to both supervisor and worker that Lisa's negative feelings about the client were influencing the interaction.

When the supervisor plays the client, she allows the worker an opportunity to try out various interventions. It is useful here to first ask the worker for her worst case scenario of client response. Often the worker is afraid to broach a difficult subject or to explore deeper for fear that the elder will become angry and break off contact, or become sad and start to cry. Simply voicing these fears is helpful. When the worker has rehearsed responding to anger and sadness, the real situation becomes easier to risk.

Line by Line

Line by Line reading is done of a section of the process recording in which the student experienced difficulty. The student reads aloud, stopping after each interaction to recollect his feelings and thoughts at the moment. Interventions are then examined, critiqued, and replayed. Finally, the student anticipates how he might respond to a similar situation the next time around.

> John returned to the point in the process when he changed the subject after Ms. P. started to complain of urinary incontinence. He recognized his embarrassment. He also realized that she was trying to resolve whether or not to have surgery and needed to discuss the pros and cons with him. With the supervisor, he figured out a variety of appropriate responses for discussing intimate matter with older female clients.

Experiential Exercises are useful for Practical Learners who are especially adept at role playing the client. Often, their greatest fear is of client anger or rejection if they do not accomplish some concrete task. For this reason, it is particularly useful for Intuitive Learners to role play such encounters from both client and worker points of view. Line by Line readings are also helpful for the Intuitive Learner, demanding that she separate her feelings from those of the client at each step of the process.

Experiential exercises are initially difficult for the Intellectual Learner. She may have trouble remembering the interaction of an interview and is often more clear about her analysis of a situation than of what actually happened. Or, she may falter over the choice of words, fearful of saying the wrong thing, even in a simulated interview. It is more productive, at first, for the Intellectual Learner to role play the client and the supervisor to play the worker. In so doing, the supervisor can demonstrate interviewing techniques while the learner views the situation from the client's perspective.

PART II
TEACHING AND APPLICATION

Chapter 4

Practice Skills I

SERVICES TO INDIVIDUALS

Practice skills used with older persons are no different than those used with other age groups. However, the special characteristics of the population demand a different application. The following discussion illustrates supervisory techniques to help the worker understand these applications.

Engagement and Contracting

The elderly are frequently alone and isolated. Often they welcome a new person into their lives and initial engagement is easy for even the neophyte social worker to accomplish.

> Mrs. L. welcomed me enthusiastically and barely listened as I identified myself as the social worker from the home health care agency. She eagerly tried to help me with my coat and offered me a piece of fruit.

The issue for supervision in this example is what constitutes engagement. Is Mrs. L. clear about the role of a home health care social worker? Is she truly so receptive when the worker addresses difficult issues? More than other populations, older people will reach out for company, but this is not engagement.

At the same time, the prevalence of physical and/or mental impairments can make a simple introduction problematic.

> Mrs. N. has been in the nursing home for three months and is paralyzed and speech impaired. I introduced myself and explained my function. Mrs. N. smiled and said "yes, yes, yes." I felt good because it sounded like she wanted help, but she suddenly began to cry and clutched my hand frantically.

In this instance, the supervisor must provide basic information about aphasia and how to determine the level of comprehension. As with hearing loss, creative interventions and a high tolerance for frustration are necessary to develop a helping relationship.

The elderly are often referred to agencies because someone close to them notices a decline in functioning of which they are not aware or accepting. In fact, reference to functional loss can be perceived as threatening. In this situation, contracting without a hidden agenda is often a serious ethical dilemma for the student or new worker.

> Mrs. Z. was referred for social service by the home care nurse because she was depressed. She insisted that she needed help only with getting Medicaid reinstated. She bristled at the word depression, insisting she wasn't crazy. In supervision, the worker worried about how to treat her when she refused treatment. The idea of initially working on the concrete needs while establishing a relationship and assessing mental status was comfortable for the worker. This plan made the contract clear and honest, but allowed for changes in the future.

In other cases, it is the worker rather than the client who has difficulty putting the presenting problem into words.

> Mr. P. was identified as a student social work case by the floor team because he had experienced a severe heart attack and the death of a roommate within one month's time. He reacted with angry, demanding behavior to staff. The team hoped that contact with a social worker would improve Mr.

P.'s behavior. The student asked for help in engaging this involuntary client. She feared that he would identify her with other staff who he saw as always trying to make him do something he didn't want to do. After a role play with the supervisor in which she put herself in the client's shoes and tried to imagine his feelings, the student was able to go in with a different approach. She acknowledged that two serious incidents had happened to him in a very short time and imagined how difficult that could be for him. He said "you wouldn't believe it" and went on to describe the night of his heart attack. At the end of the interview, they agreed that there was more to talk about before he could get "used to the changes."

With the mentally frail, the dilemma is even greater since the building of a relationship will not necessarily make the problem clearer to the client.

Mr. H., an 89-year-old nursing home resident, sometimes confused the social worker with the activity worker ("where's your guitar today?"). At other times he thought she was his daughter. It was hard for the worker to understand what would constitute a meaningful intervention when Mr. H. could not grasp her role and function. In supervision, she and her supervisor focussed on the help offered in the moment and how the confused person can value the response even when he is unclear about who offered it. They read the process recording line by line, and the student was able to identify areas where contracting could be reinforced.

Social workers new to the field of aging are initially nonplussed by the mentally impaired elder. They globally discount anything the client says as being irrational and therefore meaningless. The supervisor must help the worker recognize the difference between intellectual and emotional functioning. Even in cases of severe mental impairment, the feelings remain intact. It is to these feelings that the worker must relate.

Exploration

Exploring is designed to uncover the many factors involved in a client's presenting problem in order to understand it in depth. Exploring involves identifying what aspects of the client's story to investigate further and when to do so.

The elderly person has, of course, a longer story than other clients. The worker needs to learn how to elicit information and how to focus while still offering an empathic ear. Help is needed in identifying critical areas to explore.

Issues of independence/dependence, isolation, loss, and illness always need exploration.

> The supervisor commented to Ellen that Mrs. L. often says that she never wants to burden her son. The supervisor wondered exactly what she meant. Ellen said Mrs. L. is very independent. The supervisor agreed but suggested a role play with Ellen as Mrs. L. She asked Mrs. L. to tell her about her son. As Mrs. L., Ellen expressed some fear of "bothering" him. She also talked about her daughter-in-law and past strains in the relationship. From this exercise, Ellen began to think of issues for further exploration.

Issues of adaptation and coping are equally important because they illustrate an elder's strengths that may be mobilized to deal with current situations. Information about these strengths is often imbedded in stories from the past. The worker with no background in the meaning of life review or reminiscence to the elderly may discount such stories or cut them off to get to the real work.

> Each time Mike meets with Mr. S., he has to listen to the same story of how Mr. S. came to this country with a dollar in his pocket and retired as the president of his own business. He asked the supervisor how he could direct the interview to resolve Mr. S.'s roommate conflict. When the supervisor suggested that Mike take an opposite approach — asking Mr. S. to tell him more about the business experience — Mike was puzzled. "Isn't it an escape, wrong, to live in the past?" The supervisor asked Mike to consider why Mr. S. might keep

repeating the story. It took some time for Mike to come up with the first. "He wants to impress me?" "Yes," the supervisor said and added, "perhaps he wants you to know that he was not always a helpless old man in a nursing home." The fact that there could be more than one meaning imbedded in the story stimulated Mike to a consideration of more. "He could run a business but can't control his roommate?" "Perhaps," said the supervisor. "How could you find out?"

The key to teaching workers the skill of exploration with elders is in arousing their curiosity. Younger clients or clients presenting problems closer to those of their workers naturally inspire greater curiosity. The concerns of the elderly are assumed to be one dimensional and concrete. The supervisor can help the worker appreciate the complexity and the challenge.

Sometimes beginning workers fear exploration because it is seen as "prying." This belief is true in all fields of practice, but it is especially true in workers who have been raised to respect the aged — not to question anything they say. If this appears to be an issue, the supervisor must direct attention toward delineating between the personal and the professional self. The analogy of a physician is frequently helpful; i.e., she must ask the elder to disrobe and raise questions that would not be permissible in ordinary social relationships.

The gerontological social worker needs to learn particular aspects of the aging process that invariably need exploring in depth. She must look for the meaning behind non-verbal behavior and repetition of thoughts or incidents, which signal to the experienced practitioner that a more complex meaning is hidden in the words.

Assessment and Goal Planning

Assessment is the core of social work practice. To intervene effectively, the social worker has to understand the components that affect the elder's life. Beginning strategies of intervention are developed via what is known about the client, his history, and current situation.

Developing an assessment for the old person is, in most ways, similar to assessment of any other client. It is different in that medical and environmental content is of equal importance to psychosocial content. Further, there is much more material to be assimilated because the older person has lived longer.

The wealth of material makes it essential that the worker be able to discern patterns and determine relevance. The supervisor can help by sharpening the worker's ability to listen to themes as well as content.

> In supervision, Sarah looked at her process recording to expand her assessment of Mrs. K. Mrs. K. had a series of complaints about the poor care she received in the hospital. She added that her wishes were ignored and it was similar to a visit to her daughter who never provided good meals or a pleasant atmosphere. Sarah postulated that feeling uncared for and having unmet needs were basic themes in Mrs. K.'s life. She understood that solving the current problem would not necessarily affect the underlying problem or Mrs. K.'s feelings. This factor was significant in determining future interventions.

In addition, the assessment of the elder explores all aspects of medical history even if an impairment is not apparent. Workers new to gerontology need knowledge about the more chronic health problems, acute illnesses, accidents of elders, and usual treatments. A medical dictionary, Merck manual, and *Physicians' Desk Reference*, supplemented by hand-outs for the lay public provided by such organizations as the American Heart Association, provide a good working foundation. Contacts and collaboration with other health care professionals expand upon the information.

The assessment is usually used for care planning, whether in the community or institution. For this reason, careful attention must be paid to informal and formal supports, existing or potential, that can be utilized in the elder's behalf. Foremost, is salient information about the family (the family of origin as well as the family of mid and late life). Family history impacts heavily on the elderly person's life situation and his feelings about it. Information about neighbors, friends, and agencies involved in the elder's care round out the picture.

Typically, beginning students and workers have great difficulty separating data from opinion, and fact from inference. But it is crucial that they learn to do so. Accomplishment of this task in written form may require many attempts. The supervisor first helps the worker orally by encouraging her to back up her opinions with factual examples.

> Maryanne, a first year student, returned from her first home visit and announced to the supervisor that the client belonged in a nursing home. The supervisor responded that the mission of the agency was to keep elders in the community as long as possible. She would have done better to ask the student what she had observed that led to that conclusion. She missed the opportunity for a discussion of assessment which would teach the student to think through her opinions.

The establishment of long- and short-term goals is both the outcome and the purpose of the assessment. Goals are the expected result of the social worker's intervention—not the intervention itself. This point is often confused by workers. For example, "to establish a relationship" is not a goal but a means to an end. One establishes a relationship with a client to help him receive and use certain services or so that he can resolve certain issues.

The best goals are written in measurable terms, expected time frames, and phrased from the client's point of view. For example, Mrs. J. will find an alternative living arrangement that offers housekeeping services—6 months; Mr. W. will decide about cataract surgery—2 months. Measurable terms and expected time frames allow the supervisior and worker to monitor progress and revise case plans as necessary. Phrasing from the client's point of view keeps the worker faithful to the client's wishes rather than imposing her own. An outline form that provides subject headings helps guide the writer to appropriate content.

Ongoing Work

Ongoing work with the elderly requires that the student work with feelings on an intimate level. While dealing with painful feelings is a hard task for any practitioner, the student or worker may feel especially hopeless when confronted with multiple losses.

Jane described to her supervisor how depressed Ms. C. seemed. Jane remarked that Ms. C. would start to say something and then stop, saying "what's the point?" The supervisor asked how Jane felt about her. Jane reluctantly shared that Ms. C. did have little to look forward to, or to look back on. Jane stated that Ms. C. was right: illness and death were all that lay ahead. "So what is the point?" asked the supervisor. Jane talked about her previous job with troubled adolescents, and how there was hope no matter how bad the situation was. The supervisor asked if it felt different with Ms. C., because she was old. Jane agreed, but soon added that Ms. C. had more insight and understanding than her previous clients, and recalled illustrative incidents. The supervisior and Jane then discussed how work with Ms. C. could help her better cope with her daily life.

Except for acute care medical or psychiatric settings, most agency practice with elders is open-ended, an appropriate modality for a population whose needs often fluctuate. As a consequence, workers may focus their attention on new cases or those in which a crisis is occurring. They offer the others periodic monitoring and supportive services. The danger here is that important developments after the initial assessment may be overlooked. Or that elder and worker will reach an impasse. At this point, it is useful to return to the assessment and case plan and re-evaluate the interventive strategy.

Focussing

One problem for both worker and elder during the ongoing phase is focussing. Workers typically have difficulty structuring their contacts with clients. Often they report "the conversation turned to" or "the subject changed," as if they had no responsibility for the direction of the interview. While the client's free association may be useful in psychoanalytic practice, it is not the model for goal directed social work, especially with the elderly who have a tendency to digress. Digression may be an avoidance of discussing painful subjects. However, it is often the result of cognitive or sensory impairment, unfamiliarity with the norms of a social work interview, or social isolation and delight at having someone to talk to. The skill of maintaining focus on the work without preemptively cutting off important material that initially may sound irrelevant is difficult to achieve. The worker should use the initial and ongoing assessment as a guide. Above all, the worker must learn and feel comfortable with the words that will shift the client from an unproductive to productive pattern of thought without alienating or angering him.

> The supervisor role played with Cynthia the situation of Mrs. F. Mrs. F. hung on at the end of every interview and would not let her leave. She suggested phrases the worker might use to leave comfortably. Cynthia also used supervisory help in preparing to focus Mr. Z. who had limited hearing and sight. She learned to touch him on the arm when she wished to interject a comment or change the course of the discussion.

Special issues that often arise in the ongoing phase include the handling of reminiscence, sexuality, and death and dying. These methods are discussed in detail in Chapter 5.

Termination

Termination is often a most emotionally painful social work process. Ideally, termination is a time when the client comes to a resolution about his needs and has no further need of services. In practice, termination is often more involved with the worker's schedule and occurs with a change of job or the end of a student placement. It is not uncommon for the worker to experience guilt and anxiety about abandoning the elderly client. Because agency resources are often scarce, the worker's perception may be correct. It is likely that the client will receive less services when the worker leaves — especially if he is a student. Further, there is never a good time for a worker to terminate. Frail elderly clients are prone to emergencies that inevitably turn up as the worker is ready to broach the subject of his leaving. Of course, the aged have had much experience with loss and have developed coping strategies to accommodate to the loss of a significant person. However, the loss also conjures up painful memories.

Issues of professional parameters quickly come to the fore. Students and workers typically experience conflicts about gift giving and continued visiting or letter writing with the older person after their departure. It is helpful in supervision to focus on the end of the professional relationship. Even if the practitioner could visit regularly, the relationship has changed and is no longer the same. As the worker takes in this concept, he can focus on pieces of the relationship and how much of the relationship is involved in work issues. Student or worker can begin to share this thinking with the client: "Even if I came to visit you, I couldn't help you with changing your health aide." The student or worker will also begin to understand that visits and other communication will only disappoint the elder as a close relationship cannot usually be sustained.

Assigned readings on the meaning of termination in the therapeutic relationship are helpful. They provide departing staff with a conceptual understanding of the impact of their departure on clients and themselves. The supervisor can follow up by helping the worker anticipate how the news of termination will affect each of his clients. An individualized approach and time table for working it through can be implemented.

The student or worker is also terminating with the supervisor. The supervisor's role-modelling of how one says goodbye in a professional relationship will underscore the importance of reviewing and coming to terms with the relationship. These actions allow both parties the freedom to move on.

SERVICES TO FAMILIES

The new worker may harbor many myths and stereotypes about the elderly population. One of the most damaging assumptions is that older people are abandoned by their adult children, who dump them into nursing homes at the first sign of frailty. The actuality, borne out by three decades of research, is that placement is turned to as a last resort by overwhelmed families who have tried other arrangements. When a family member applies to an agency for services for his parents, the worker will recognize the concern. However, she usually accepts at face value the statement that other siblings are unable or unwilling to participate in caregiving. Similarly, when the elder is seen alone at intake, workers may not question the wish not to bother grown children"who have their own lives."

Less common but equally destructive myths may be held about family relationships in late life. For example, that suicidal ideation after the death of a spouse of 55 years is rational because "life is over" for the survivor, or that aged siblings are too debilitated to offer much to the elder. Sisters and brothers who have been estranged for many years often become re-engaged at a time in life when all hold more in common than they have since childhood. Widows can and do find meaning and even joy in life when the acute mourning period is over. The potential of support by siblings, nieces, and nephews may be overlooked by younger workers not accustomed to exploring these relationships.

Teaching work with families is a sequential educational process. It begins by promoting attitudinal changes within the worker and leads to enhanced assessment and intervention skills.

One exercise is particularly effective in small groups (and can profitably be incorporated into orientation curricula) but can be used individually as well. Rather than citing dry statistics about family involvement in late life, the worker can be asked to think of a grandparent and list all the relatives involved. She can then be asked to calculate the travel time between each person and the elder as well as the frequency of contact. In a surprisingly high number of cases, the worker's individual experience will reflect national statistics; but she will think that her family is different. A selected reading list is a good adjunct to such a discussion, but photocopied articles have a greater likelihood of being read. Some fictional accounts of late life families also have a powerful effect on more literary minded workers.

Once the worker has begun thinking in terms of family with every case, she must make individualized assessments of her clients. The genogram is a useful tool that can be used with alert elders as a part of the interventive process. The worker can use it to order the family information already known and determine areas requiring further exploration.

After the involved and potentially involvable family members are identified, it is helpful to explore the worker's perception of each one's stake in the care plan of the elder. Frequently, what will emerge are worker judgements based on positions expressed to her. For example, she may be biased, favoring the housewife daughter who wishes to keep the mother in the community and against the working daughter who is pushing for placement. These judgements lurk just below the level of consciousness and often unwittingly influence worker interactions with family members. They should be openly expressed and examined.

Multiple identifications and finding commonalities in conflictual situations are crucial to the success of family work with the elderly. These techniques can usefully be practiced within the supervisory conference.

One approach is to ask the worker for the message behind each position — the underlying content beneath the spoken message. For example, the working daughter's position may be that mother should enter a nursing home she will pay for. Her message may be that she would feel less worried when she is away on a trip. The housewife daughter's message may be that she would feel more secure about her mother if she can maintain control over her diet by bringing over foods she has prepared. Differences in position need not become a power struggle if the worker can underscore commonalities in the message. In this case, both daughters are concerned and wish to contribute what they can. When both daughters and mother hear this from the worker, they are on the way to finding a mutually satisfactory plan.

Another approach to teaching work with families is an experiential exercise in which the worker is asked to pretend that she is each family member and voice their concerns about the central issue.

While raising worker self-awareness prior to meeting with families is essential, a successful encounter is not assured. Often the worker may feel intimidated; by individual family members who are perceived as powerful authority figures or simply by conducting a group interview. She may also be confused as to where her primary allegiance lies — elder *or* the family. She also may fear breaching confidentially. Or, she may anticipate the displeasure of one family member if she plans a conference to include others of whom he has spoken his disapproval. For these reasons, the supervisor can never assume that the worker with a sound assessment can move easily into the intervention.

Preparation for the family meeting should center upon as accurate a prediction as possible of what might occur. Surprisingly, it does not matter if this prediction is borne out in the ensuing contact. The worker who is well prepared for several contingencies has developed a sense of confidence and flexibility that can serve her well when the unexpected arises.

Ms. W., a 23-year-old first year graduate student in the hospital's neurological unit, had to meet with her 92-year-old client's two nieces and their husbands. They had come from out of town to discuss care plans after her severely disabling stroke. She was overwhelmed because all four were middle-aged professional people; two with administrative positions in health agencies. The supervisor helped the worker anticipate this family's need for full information about options before making a decision. Marshalling of all the resources and the pros and cons of each helped the worker feel more secure. She also realized that she lacked sufficient understanding of the prognosis and sought clarification from the staff physician. She secured his availability to speak to the family if necessary. The supervisor advised her to concentrate on the messages beneath the positions and to reach for negatives before assuming consensus. Most important the worker was reminded that she did not have responsibility for the decision; that was with the family. She did, however, have responsibility for ensuring the best process possible. The interview turned out differently than had been anticipated by either supervisor or student in that one niece began by saying that she had washed her hands of all responsibility, to the shock and dismay of her sister. The men sat helplessly quiet. The worker had to switch gears immediately, abandoning all that she had prepared. However, she proved well able to mediate the family conflicts and emerge with a viable plan for the aunt. She remembered that it was the family's job to come up with a plan and her job to give them the information and facilitate their decision.

Whenever possible, elders should be present in any family meetings in which their fate is decided. Families may need time alone first to plan how to orchestrate this participation.

In cases, as the above, the elder may be too incapacitated to participate in a family meeting. The worker must be reminded that it is her responsibility to speak for the elder's point of view and report back to the elder (with or without the family) what has transpired.

Supervisory time going over the intricacies of one such encounter should be enough. However, there should be the expectation that the worker will be able to translate the principles to similar situations. Readings are especially helpful as an adjunct to preparation for family encounters. As with most reading assigned in supervision, this should be practical rather than theoretical. Interview transcripts, audio-visuals, or practice texts that focus on case examples are most apt to be used.

SERVICES TO GROUPS

Many of the most common problems encountered by the elderly can be addressed by the provision of group work services. Groups not only offer much touted socialization opportunities, but provide members with a forum to share common concerns, provide and receive aid from peers, and assume new roles.

Many agencies oriented to the provision of individual services are resistant to the institution of group work for the elderly. Administrators often fear that organizing elders will result in a challenge to the agency structure. Workers are often unfamiliar or unskilled in the group treatment modality. Transportation is a major issue in the community where many potential participants cannot travel independently to get to the agency. While the nursing home would appear to be an ideal setting for group work services, the extreme cognitive and mental deficits of many residents require worker creativity and commitment. Groups require the worker to make a major investment of time to plan, recruit, and run the group. However, once formed, groups provide a cost-effective and caring agency response to the needs of many elders. The following in-depth discussion of groups is presented to encourage supervisors to incorporate this modality into their agencies.

The group modality of service comes in many shapes and sizes. Often a creative combination best meets the need of the aging population in a particular setting. A first consideration that shapes group organization is purpose: What common need is shared by all potential participants?

The following are some types of groups:

Task-Centered Groups are extremely useful in congregate living and senior centers as a vehicle for enabling elders to assume maximum control over the decisions that affect their lives. Governing councils, social action groups, newsletter groups, and activity planning groups are a few examples of this form.

Mutual Aid Groups are generally organized to address a particular difficulty shared by all the members, such as a group for recent widows or families of Alzheimer's patients. Members share their experiences and receive practical suggestions and emotional support from their peers. Reminiscence groups are a form of a mutual aid group in which members foster and enhance the recollections of each other. This forum affirms the unique importance of each life.

Program Groups (also known as *Activity Groups*) occupy a professional domain between Recreational Therapy, and Social Work. The goal of the group, rather than the organizing theme, determines which profession is equipped to lead. Often, it is simply a matter of emphasis. For example, a reality orientation, current events, or poetry writing group might be run as a class, in which mastery of the material is of primary importance. Content is secondary to the interactional process and fostering of relationship skills. Thus, the goal of the group will determine which professional is the best leader.

Students and workers can be encouraged to use their skills and talents to develop a group service for the aged. Groups utilizing poetry, art, drama, pets, etc., have the potential of providing elders with new skills and means of communicating with others. The worker also finds the experience satisfying and productive.

The student or worker who gravitates to group services is frequently attracted by the measure of control not found in the one-to-one encounter. She may lapse into the teacher role with an overemphasis on product and insufficient attention to process. For example, poetry groups have been notably successful with elderly, to whom poetry is a foreign experience, as long as the worker focusses on the feelings the poetry elicits rather than on the quality of the poems.

Mentally frail elders may have difficulty in a current events group but respond appropriately and enjoy a reminiscence group. Current events groups are very successful with the elderly if the worker understands the need to identify issues that are most meaningful to this population — changes in social security payments, legislation for the elderly. Such groups can help the older person connect a current experience to his past.

> Mark read an article in the newspaper about the troubles in the Mid-East. He asked Mr. K. if he had ever been in the service. Mr. K., a proud ex-marine, talked about his experience and contrasted it with present-day terrorism.

The decision for a *time limited* versus an *open-ended group* should ideally be guided by the group purpose and the members' needs. However, like so many other professional decisions, it is more often a compromise necessitated by agency structure and workers' schedules.

Time-limited groups are, not surprisingly, best suited to time-limited situations. Six to twelve weeks can be extremely useful to recent retirees, new residents groups, or bereavement groups or for planning specific actions. As with short-term individual work, time limits provide a focus and urgency for leaders and participants alike. Members must make a commitment to such a group at the outset. There is no time to integrate new members. There is also the ever-present danger of attrition, leading to disintegration of the group before its planned termination. Because health and transportation problems often interfere with elders' regular attendance in groups, it is wise to plan on a group of twelve members to ensure six to eight at each meeting.

Open-ended groups, with comparatively fluid membership, are

best suited to the fluctuating health and life circumstances of the frail elderly.

While group service can provide some of the most satisfying service to the elderly, it can also produce anxiety for the student or worker. Facing a group of elderly people can make even the most experienced pratitioner nervous.

A fear for the worker about groups is the basic "more of them than of me" feeling and a loss of control. An inept intervention which can potentially be glossed over in private becomes a public issue. A broken counselling appointment may be disappointing. A group to which no one comes is a disaster. Some of the handicaps common in the elderly, such as hearing problems or mild confusion, are seen by beginners as monumental roadblocks in beginning a group service. For this reason, the support and active involvement of the supervisor is necessary throughout the process.

STAGES OF GROUP PROCESS

Beginnings, ongoing work, and termination are clearly delineated phases of group work. Each poses special challenges and opportunities for the gerontological social work supervisor teaching specific skills to the student or worker.

Beginnings

Knowing what to expect and anticipatory empathy ("tuning in") are steps most helpful to group leaders as they begin. If possible, it is best to have the practitioner participate actively in the first phases of group formation. In some cases, they may identify a common need or interest among a few individual clients that could be generalized to other elders.

> Mark had three male clients in the nursing home. All loved to engage him in political discussions and lamented that none of the "old women" shared this interest. Mark realized that current events groups sponsored by the recreation department did not meet the deeper needs of these men. They wished to review and validate their past life experiences, to express their

anger at a changing world, to exercise their wits and tongues on something more substantial than the next national holiday, to assert their masculine identity in a predominantly female setting. Mark's supervisor helped him to articulate a profile of older men who might benefit from such a service and encouraged him to contact the recreation leader about possible referrals.

For the supervisor to identify a group need, she must have, and communicate to the group leaders, a clear idea of what the service is about. "Support group" or "group to discuss issues of aging" is not a clearly-defined service. The group leaders will not be able to explain the service, and group members will not understand it.

The group must be responsive to an identified need. Thinking out the purpose of the group and the identified need can be a part of the tuning in process. The supervisor needs to be sure that the group leader understands the purpose of the group. In the beginning, the supervisor encourages the leader to consider how the members might receive the offer of group service.

> Beginning with a group of recent widows connected to a senior center, Katherine worked on the "tuning in" with her supervisor. Katherine thought that women would be uncomfortable talking about the loss of their spouses with strangers. She also imagined that they would probably be reluctant to hear sad stories and would feel worse afterward. Katherine and her supervisor worked on how to verbalize some of these concerns to the group. The supervisor also identified some of these concerns as belonging to Katherine herself.

Many older people have no prior group experience and need much encouragement to participate. It is not sufficient to post a notice or make an announcement and expect a group to appear at the appointed hour. Even elders who initially express interest may drop out before the first meeting. This response can discourage even the most enthusiastic worker.

Individual meetings with potential group members thus serve a vital purpose for elders and leaders. Elders have a chance to ask questions and express expectations and reservations in a nonthreatening environment. Often they do not come to the group's first meeting unless they have a prior connection to the leader.

Exploring elder concerns within the group itself is difficult. The leader may fear that negative feelings will result in the group coming apart.

> If Katherine asked how group members felt about sharing their losses, she feared that they might react negatively to hearing tales of woe. The supervisor asked what she would do if that happened. She said that she would explore more. The supervisor agreed. She suggested that Katherine focus on what happened when they tried to discuss their losses with family or friends.

In beginning, a group leader needs reassurance that exploration will not mean the end of the group and negative reactions will not reflect poorly on her. In addition, actual experience will illustrate the positive outcome of exploration.

Contracting around group services should come naturally from the tuning in process and sound exploration. The group leader needs to see the contract as both a statement of purpose and an ongoing process. How the group views itself and how members interact with each other is a dynamic process that has to be continually reviewed.

> Katherine described the upset she felt when Mrs. J. and Mrs. K. got into an argument. Mrs. K. accused Mrs. J. of being a chronic complainer. Katherine had tried to mediate the dispute, but felt she had only cut them off. The supervisor suggested it was a contracting problem. She wondered if in the mediation process, Katherine could focus on both women's understanding of the purpose of the group. The need was to help each understand what constitutes legitimate discussion and involve other group members.

Ongoing Work

Ongoing phases require understanding of group dynamics and various group phenomena. As the group progresses, the supervisor helps the leader understand the process. Scapegoating, resistance to staying with the work, and premature agreement really do occur in groups with the elderly as they do with other populations. However, in groups with the elderly, some of these processes are played out in frequently unrecognized ways. For example, scapegoating will often focus on the mentally frail participant who embodies the worst fears of the more able members.

A common form of resistance involves focussing on positives of the recent past. For example, a student who inherits a group from another student will find that group members focus on how much more, able, healthy, intellectually stimulating, jovial, close-knit, etc., this group was previously. The new leader needs to understand this resistance for what it is and not feel demoralized by constant references to a glorified past.

Termination

The termination process has special implications for the elderly. It occurs at a time of loss in the life cycle and also reawakens earlier losses. In addition, the ending of the group may mean the end of agency service. Painful feelings may get displaced: decreasing attendance, minimizing the usefulness of the group, or arguing among members are not uncommon. The leader may detach from the group, feeling that it is pointless to pursue proper closure.

The supervisor must demand a termination process that validates the service and involves the members in an appropriate ending. The leader's hesitancy may involve an underlying fear that the service was indeed worthless. She may believe that any exploration of negatives or review of process will result in confirmation of that fear.

It is crucial that the student or worker believe in the process of termination. By carrying through the process he will learn that endings are hard, and that people often respond to pain with anger and rejection. Once again, the issue is role modeling. If the supervisor allows the leader to let the group come apart, she communicates the sense that the service was indeed meaningless. Exploration of termination issues is confidence building to the leader, and crucial to an understanding of underlying group dynamics.

Chapter 5

Practice Skills II

INTERDISCIPLINARY COLLABORATION/TEAM WORK

Collaborative work represents possibly the greatest challenge in the practitioner's experience. However, the experience will vary depending on whether the practitioner is a student or worker. Here we discuss both similarities and differences.

The Student

From the average client's point of view, the student is *the* helping person. Although the elderly person is told that the worker is a student, it usually does not mean much. When working with other disciplines, however, the student is *always* in the student role. Often this works to his advantage — the professionals will sometimes spend extra time giving fuller explanations of an issue or provide an unsolicited learning piece. However, it also means that the student has the least status, limited influence and minimal power to change a situation.

Students in larger agencies such as hospitals or nursing homes, especially where there are multidisciplinary teams, learn early about systems. They are often shocked to discover the complexity of the system and their minor role in it. It is always useful for the supervisor's beginning educational assessment to learn how the student approaches team members. Bright, otherwise able students may be intimidated by a brusque physician, or an unfriendly nurse. They may limit intervention to areas not involved in another discipline's expertise. Conversely, otherwise well-mannered students may see their roles as social workers as requiring them to take an aggressive stance with other disciplines. Neither extreme serves the client's or the student's best interest. The student will need to learn how to work within the client's system, and how to interact productively with other professions.

It is particularly important when working in a multidisciplinary setting to help the student see the setting in relation to the client. The student begins to conceptualize her role better if she understands that the client has a relationship to each of the disciplines involved in his care. The relationship between client and other disciplines may be impaired, but it does exist.

> Linda, a beginning student in a hospital assigned to geriatric psychiatry, expressed outrage to her supervisor about a physician's cavalier attitude. He had told her client, Mrs. M., that her joint pains were because of old age. Mrs. M. seemed even more depressed and Linda was very angry. The supervisor spoke to Linda about the physician and his probable frustration as a medical doctor on a floor where the patients had emotional problems. Linda agreed. She mentioned that Mrs. M. was even more distressed because the physician had helped her so much when she had had pneumonia during a previous admission. Supervision then focussed on the mutual disappointment of Mrs. M. and her physician and what steps Linda could take to intervene. She acted on her supervisor's suggestion that she ask the physician to explain arthritis in the elderly. She would use the opportunity to share Mrs. M.'s upset reaction with him.

Students also commonly encounter elderly clients who complain bitterly about staff, but also resist change.

> Michael arranged a meeting with the charge nurse on a nursing home floor with Mr. R. who previously had complained of long waits for care and rude treatment by nursing assistants. At the meeting, Michael was chagrined to find Mr. R. denied any complaints and assured the nurse that he had no problems on the floor. In supervision Michael identified possible reasons for this encounter. He believed Mr. R. feared reprisals. Michael understood his need to explore more before rushing to a solution. The supervisor also suggested that complaints must be investigated but often mask feelings of despair and loneliness.

Learning to consider simultaneously two possibilities — that there may be a concrete problem and that the complaints may address a more complex emotional issue — is important to working successfully in the system. When the student understands this, he understands systems well.

The disciplines that constitute the client system are not also clients. They have not sought nor identified the need for social work services. However, social work skills can and should be used to engage other disciplines in providing service for the agency's client population.

> Linda was exasperated at a team meeting. When Mrs. M.'s name came up, the physician and nurse mocked her complaining behavior. However, she listened quietly and mentioned that Mrs. M. often made her angry as well. In supervision, Linda explained that she wanted to make the discussion more constructive by understanding her colleagues' frustration. Allowing for some ventilation helped her to move the group toward problem solving. Her supervisor said that she had learned a lot about systems quickly.

Team meetings provide a special opportunity for the student to learn about collaborative work and systems intervention. Many team members participate reluctantly in the team and minimize its impact. Although usually not the team leader, the social worker often has the greatest commitment to the team process, and the skill to help the team become a functioning group.

A student participating in a team will learn from the experienced worker or from supervision to identify the common issues for team work. Sharing information, identifying cross-discipline concerns, and problem solving are all areas where the group can work together. The forum can also provide a learning experience for each discipline as they learn about each other's roles.

For the student, the team is potentially a stimulating experience. He will have many opportunities to expand his knowledge base. He may have to utilize experienced social work staff to help him influence other group members and seek supervisory help to develop skills for effective intervention. However, the opportunity to watch other disciplines operate as a unit is one of the finest learning experiences a field placement can provide.

In smaller agencies or social service agencies where other disciplines are not employed, teaching the skills of collaborative work is harder. The student does not have as much opportunity for good will built up through personal acquaintance. As a social work student on the telephone trying to reach a community physician, his status is even lower. The student must continue to focus on the common themes among the disciplines.

> John, a social work student in a community service agency, reached Mr. S.'s physician after four tries. He explained that he was working with Mr. S. on taking medication and that if he knew about his medication and overall condition he could assist in Mr. S.'s compliance with the doctor's orders.

In defining skills needed for both in-house and community collaborative work, it is useful for the student to consider the role of the other professional: what his view of the service is, and how he interacts with the client. It also is important to help students assess the impact of the particular person in the client's life. A home health aide may, for example, seem less than ideal to a student who would like the elder to have a more lively, friendlier, and intellectually stimulating individual. However, the aide may be the person keeping the client out of a nursing home. The client may appropriately view her as the mainstay of her existence. The student then needs to consider the client need, available resources, and level of service currently provided.

The Worker

The worker may have more agency sanction, but experience similar struggles in the system. She may have even more difficulty since she does not elicit the desire to help that students may arouse in other professionals. She is a team player who may, by virtue of her responsibility to promote the client's point of view, become at times an outcast on the team. She may have the respect and confidence of her colleagues in general. However, she may ruin a good "paper" care plan by reminding her colleagues that Mr. S. will never agree to the treatment. In collaborative work, the social worker learns to explore many different ideas, always willing to modify her own viewpoint but ready to risk the anger of the other collaborators to protect the client.

She can expect to spend a substantial amount of her direct practice time in contacts with people other than her elderly clients. Family members, neighbors, physicians, home care workers, and landlords are but a few of the collateral contacts with whom the worker must interact to ensure the best care for the elder.

In contrast to teaching the skills of work with individuals, the skills of mediation and advocacy are frequently overlooked in the supervision of direct practice. However, they actually require a more complex conceptual understanding and a broader range of interventive techniques.

A supervisor may suggest that the worker involve the family, get in touch with the landlord, or work with the doctor, assuming that the purpose and content of such contacts is understood. Failure of the worker to follow through or a botched encounter requiring extensive remedial action are often first signs that the message is not understood.

Time spent exploring the worker's ideas and anticipating the encounter is time well spent. Frequently, the worker has unexpressed reservations because of confusion about what constitutes confidentiality. She may be misapplying a psychoanalytic model of practice, focussing on the client-worker relationship as the unit of attention, rather than viewing her work in a systems perspective. That is not to say there cannot or should not be confidential material between elder and worker. Rather, those problems of elder functioning that involve other people are more likely to be resolved with those people present.

Skills of mediation, brokerage, and advocacy have common and specific properties. They have in common the necessity for multiple identification; the ability to empathize with several, often contradictory, views of a problem. Moreover, they frequently require a more direct, assertive stance than is usually practiced in the one-to-one therapeutic encounter. They also call upon a knowledge base that moves beyond individual psychodynamics to an understanding of systems theory as it applies to family composition, organizational development, and community organization. Finally, work with collaterals in direct practice makes professional and personal demands.

The worker must be comfortable enough in her role to be challenged. She also must be able to tolerate the ambiguity of unresolved situations. None of this comes naturally, any more than work with clients comes naturally. Workers gain competence from the opportunity to work through generic and specific issues of each modality in supervision.

MEDIATION

While work with families is a type of mediation, it is differentiated from work with the formal system by the intimate relationships and long history that exist between the elder and the informal system. With no such history, the worker is at once liberated and challenged.

The need for mediation between elders and the formal system prototypically comes into play in cases of non-compliance with health care directives.

> Mrs. L., an obese, 87-year-old diabetic widow, confessed to the worker that she frequently cheats on her diet. Her justification: "what else do I have in life to enjoy?" The fact that she had pledged the worker not to tell her doctor only became known to the supervisor when the client became an emergency admission to the hospital in a diabetic coma, and the worker came to her in the throes of guilt. Upon exploration, the worker said that since she had agreed with her client that she was entitled to pleasure in food, she felt it wrong to argue with her.

This explanation tipped the supervisor off to the dearth of interventive options that the worker had at her disposal and the necessity for teaching skills of mediation. After Mrs. L.'s recovery, they planned a meeting with Mrs. L., the doctor, the hospital nutritionist, and the worker to determine follow-up care.

The supervisor began by exploring the worker's feelings about speaking to other health care professionals and learned that she frequently felt inadequate. She did not understand medical terms nor how to respond when told that people were too busy to speak with her.

Her first assignment was reading on diabetes in material published for the layperson. Her supervisor assured her that she needed no more medical knowledge to converse effectively. Secondly, the supervisor gave her some phrases to use when she felt "brushed off" by other professionals. For example, "I know from the past that Mrs. L. will be unable to follow your diabetic regimen without further discussion with you. Since you are busy now, could you please tell me what would be a more convenient time for me to speak with you?" While it wasn't important, or even desirable, that the worker repeat these words verbatim, possessing them gave her a sense of comfort and direction.

The worker was advised to meet with each person individually beforehand. She helped Mrs. L. rehearse telling the doctor and nutritionist how hard it was for her to deny herself sweets. She also helped draw up a list of questions relating to dietary restrictions. She clued the doctor and nutritionist in to what they might expect and got a feeling for how they would respond.

An hour before the meeting, she entered the supervisor's office in a panic. What if, after all this, Mrs. L. could not comply with the diet? What if Mrs. L. is too frightened to speak? What if the doctor is curt and unsympathetic as he has been in the past? The supervisor reminded her that her job was to help the parties communicate. She also reminded her of the skills of individual work that could be translated to this new situation. The worker was reassured to learn that not all skills of mediation were foreign to her. She had mastered some in previous situations. She was also reassured to hear that whatever the outcome of the meeting, it was not the last word on the subject. At the very least, she would have laid the groundwork for Mrs. L.'s continued dialogue with those involved in her health care.

This supervisor's strategies in teaching the skills of mediation ran the gamut from didactic, advice giving, reaching for worker responses, experiential exercise, and appropriate reassurance and expectations. She recognized that the lessons would have to be reenforced before being internalized by the worker. She looked for other cases in the workload where similar interventions would be effective and challenged the worker to undertake them.

ADVOCACY

On the surface, advocacy is the easiest of direct practice skills with collaterals to master. All one must do is speak for the elderly client. This stance comes naturally to the caring worker—whatever her level of experience or skill. In fact, advocacy requires a rather sophisticated repertoire of skills. The primary one is knowing when not to use it.

Advocacy is an approach best tried when mediation has failed. Mediation validates and reconciles divergent points of view. There are no winners or losers at the end. Mediation is the intervention of choice with both informal and formal systems. It initiates future productive communication among all parties concerned. This method provides conflict resolution without a loss of face on either side.

Advocacy sets up a win-lose situation between the social worker and the target of her intervention. The social worker may well win her point. However, she may sacrifice a future relationship. Members of the interdisciplinary team who suffer a loss of face are less prone to cooperate on succeeding cases. The social worker who loses her point suffers a loss of credibility on future issues. Advocacy, then, is most appropriate and effective either as a last-resort measure or when dealing with people or organizations not likely to be encountered on an ongoing basis.

The supervisor has two teaching tasks in advocacy: to help the worker avoid precipitous, inappropriate actions and to become aware of advocacy potential.

At their first meeting, Bob told his supervisor that he wanted to work in a nursing home because he felt so bad reading about all the abuses that took place there against helpless old people. He went on at length about their need for respect and care. As the supervisor listened, she realized that he would need specific preparation before being assigned to a nursing unit. She could foresee him lecturing nurses and aides on their obligations, rendering himself ineffective in future legitimate claims on their attention. The supervisor accredited his wishes to help while pointing out that he could see situations on the unit that might confirm his expectations. How did he think he would handle it? Bob replied that is exactly why he was there, to make the situation better. The supervisor responded that he could best do that in the beginning by making notes of all his observations to discuss with her. Together, they would decide how he could best approach making necessary changes. This suggestion satisfied the student's need to do something immediately while preventing a precipitous advocacy position.

Jane entered supervision depressed about the news she had just heard. Nurses planned to move Mr. P. who she had admitted one week earlier to a nursing unit for confused residents. They claimed that his behavior was inappropriate, reflecting a level of mental impairment that could not be managed in a more independent setting. The behavior in question was flirting and suggestive gestures to female residents and staff. Jane knew his history as a traveling salesman and the recent death of his wife. She believed that he was not impaired, just responding to the newness of the situation with behaviors from the past. Now it was too late. He would be moved and deteriorate further. Jane said perhaps this work is not for her, it is just too sad to see what happens to people in nursing homes. The supervisor asked if she had spoken up about what she knew of her client in the team meeting where his fate was decided. She replied, "No, what good would it do? I am just a student. They wouldn't listen." The supervisor suggested that the student get all her facts down on paper so they could go over them together. Next, they strategized how she could call an ad hoc meeting to present the new evidence. Jane would ask for a stay of the move for a month. During this time she would work with Mr. P. intensively to orient him to the expectations of the facility. She also would be available to the nurses for consultation on how to handle him. The plan was accepted by the team. With the supervisor's help, the student was empowered to advocate for her client successfully.

SPECIAL ISSUES

Life Review

In the past several years, life review has been popularized in the literature and designated as therapeutic for the elderly. Indeed, all evidence supports the process of life review to integrate the events of one's past and move successfully into the final stage of life.

New workers often respond to life review in one of two ways. Either they see reflections on the past as characteristic of the elderly and discount them. Or they steep themselves in material on life review and encourage reminiscing as the main thrust of their work.

Elderly people often do enjoy talking about the past, but do not necessarily need the social worker to help them reminisce. The worker needs to use reminiscing as a tool rather than as an end in and of itself.

The understanding of why and when reminiscing should be encouraged is a key learning task. It is useful to first help the worker identify what the elder's present day problems are. Reminiscence can then be directed to a past coping pattern that can be utilized in the present. Reminiscence can also be directed to long-held attitudes that might be presenting obstacles in the present situation.

Mrs. D., an 82-year-old woman, was referred to a service agency for help with Medicaid and food stamp applications. Each time she met with the worker she spoke repeatedly about the application, but didn't work on it. One day, the worker asked her about the Great Depression and how it affected Mrs. D. and her family. Mrs. D. told a compelling story of coping with adversity in the 1930s and of all the dreams she could not realize. She talked contemptuously of those who gave up. The worker then asked if government help felt like giving up to her. Mrs. D. responded that she had no choice, but it did. They continued to talk into the next week about the WPA and other subsidy programs. Mrs. D. was then able to submit the documentation and complete the application.

When inappropriately applied by overzealous workers, reminiscence can be patronizing and may preclude work that has more meaning to their present-day lives.

Mary attended a workshop on Life Review and returned full of enthusiasm to start such a group in the senior citizen housing project where she worked. Participation dropped after the first two weeks, and she was encouraged by her supervisor to follow-up with members to find out why. Several responded that they were too preoccupied with crime and other community problems in the neighborhood to "live in the past." Mary took the hint and re-contracted with the group. It became a place to discuss current life problems and share solutions. Increased attendance and spirited discussion ensued as the members were helped to help each other cope.

Life review may raise complex themes. An older person who sacrificed her own needs may be expressing her fear of dependence and her struggle to cope with the aging process. The confused ex-vaudevillian who can remember the minor stars of the Ziegfield Follies is also conveying his uniqueness and specialness.

The supervisor with an understanding of the aging population can help the student understand the assessment and interventive significance of reminiscence in the same way that he would assess acting out behavior in adolescence. The memories of the elderly help us identify the struggles of their existence as well as the strengths they draw upon.

Sexuality

Perhaps no aspect of work with the elderly elicits more discomfort than issues of sexuality. Evidence of an elderly person's interest in sex, not to mention active participation, is enough to generate embarrassment among those around them, including professional workers. The view of sex as the domain of the young, and the belief that interest in sex atrophies as the body ages is now an antiquated one. In real life, however, Victorian principles have more influence among the aged than many of us acknowledge.

To understand sexual needs as an important, often unfulfilled, area in the life of an elderly person is a part of a full assessment. Similarly, deviant sexual behavior needs to be put into the context of the elderly person's life patterns. In this way, interventions can be geared toward helping rather than labelling.

A couple in a nursing home, for example, may be laughed at and ostracized for public displays of affection when the home does not offer space for private meetings. A home attendant may need help to understand that an elderly man's masturbation is a common practice. She is only aware of it because of her proximity to the client as well as his sensory losses which make him unaware of her presence.

On the other hand, the gerontological practitioner needs to look carefully at the more liberal view of sex and the old person. Sexual interest is more acceptable and common for the elderly than it was in decades past. Nevertheless, there is still a significant decrease in sexual activity. Discomfort talking about sex is neither uncommon nor surprising in this generation who came of age before the sexual revolution.

The worker will need to understand that the same elderly client who will bare her soul talking about her daughter's emotional problems may be horrified at the mere mention of sex. The worker may need to discuss sex with an elder if there is evidence of some problems in this area. She should proceed with delicacy and in the context of the presenting problem.

> The supervisor sent a student to do a home visit on a couple self-referred for home attendant services. She was shocked to pick up the process recording and find that the entire interview had centered on the changing sexual relationship of the couple since the husband's recent stroke. The student said that she had focused on the topic because she had noticed that they had separate bedrooms since the stroke and decided to explore the meaning to them. She noted they were "a little uncomfortable" but felt they needed the opportunity to express their feelings. She needed supervisory help to recognize that explora-

tion on this first interview could more productively focus on the reason they were requesting agency services.

At the same time, the supervisor needs to be alert for the worker who is uncomfortable in this area.

Judith, a recent graduate who came from an Orthodox Jewish family, took a job in an agency providing mental health services. She was counseling Mrs. L., an elderly woman whose husband had died three months earlier. She was dumbfounded when Mrs. L. expressed her regret that regular sexual contact was over. In supervision, she and her supervisor discussed Mrs. L.'s bohemian background and sexual attitudes in contrast to Judith's parochial orientation. At their next meeting, Judith complimented Mrs. L. on her ability to verbalize her concern. Then she suggested they work on Mrs. L.'s sense of loss and unmet needs.

Finally, the supervisor herself is not exempt from some discomfort in this area.

Allan mentioned Mrs. R. and Mr. F., a couple in a nursing home. Their request to share a room had the staff in an uproar. The supervisor surprised Allan by shrugging off the issue. When pressed she recommended no intervention. Allan asked how he could do that. Then the supervisor realized her own inhibitions were interfering with the expectation that Allan explore this request as he would any other and deal with staff attitudes.

Homosexuality among the aged is an issue that often arouses judgmental feelings on the part of supervisors and workers. Aging homosexuals often have a greater need for social work intervention. They are usually childless and so less likely to have family supports. However, older gay men and lesbian women often have a support network of friends who function as surrogate family.

Homosexuals may have special financial problems because pensions, OASI of life partners are not available to them as they would be for a spouse. In addition, they have lived a lifetime of sexual nonacceptance which may foster secretiveness, anger, and anxiety. Supervisors and workers must be sensitive to the unspoken messages of single older people who often present their needs in veiled terms.

Mr. P., a 71-year-old retired music teacher, attended a day program for the visually-impaired elderly. He told everyone that he boarded in a house owned by another man. When this landlord died suddenly he came to the program director asking for help finding another living arrangement. As she explored further Mr. P. told her how bereft he was. This man had been his "best friend," "psychiatrist," and "brother." As the worker encouraged him to speak more, she realized that the death, for him, was the loss of a spouse. She understood the special anguish he felt at being unable to grieve publicly. Although he eventually told the director that he had lived as a homosexual all his adult life, he asked that she not tell others at the center who "would not understand." This experience raised the director's consciousness to the importance of recognizing and legitimizing non-family relationships of her older clients and helping her staff to do so.

Death and Dying

Death is usually the most frightening issue presented by the aged. Workers may be separated from their clients by two generations. The fact that the elder may have already lived beyond normal life expectancy and could die at any time can be frightening to the novice practitioner. Discussions about death and dying can be quite overwhelming. The older person, on the other hand, may be preoccupied with illness and death. He may bring it up frequently, almost casually, in conversation.

There is much useful literature on death and dying. The supervisor may have to restrain herself from inundating the worker with too much information. Instead, she will want to focus on an understanding of the issues that may arise and of behaviors and attitudes that may accompany them.

This method will help the worker understand what the elder is trying to say and respond accordingly.

Mr. S., an 86-year-old childless widower, persisted in asking the worker to check and re-check his burial arrangements with his lawyer. He resisted efforts to talk about his underlying fears. In supervision, the worker was encouraged to explore Mr. S.'s past and focus less on fears of death. In discussing this past, it became apparent that Mr. S. was the dependable relative in his family who made all the arrangements for everyone. Now there was no one left to arrange for him after he died. An arrangement with a funeral home for a prepaid funeral lessened his anxiety.

Feelings of helplessness as the elder's life comes to an end can be worked on in supervision:

When Mrs. N. was hospitalized and near death, Andrea told her supervisor how uncomfortable she felt visiting her. Andrea felt she just sat there while the medical staff cared for Mrs. N. They talked about what Mrs. N. wanted at this point. Andrea felt she wanted someone who would listen to her and tell her the truth. Armed with the knowledge that Mrs. N. needed someone who would not deny her present state, Andrea was able to "just sit" with her.

No amount of reading and lectures will make work with the sick and dying easy. These are the most painful and frightening areas for any practitioner. The supervisor who can listen to such difficulties and provide needed support can make an enormous difference in how the practitioner manages the process.

PART III
EDUCATIONAL AND ADMINISTRATIVE SUPERVISION

Chapter 6

Educational Supervision

Agencies take on the education of students to increase services to clients, add to agency prestige, and develop supervisory skills of their workers.

In educational supervision, the agency is the laboratory in which the supervisor employs her skills to train students for the profession. The excitement in gerontological social work education is that so much of the practice is in the pioneer stage. Something new is uncovered all the time, and fresh conceptual and practice approaches are springing up from unexpected sources. Highly experienced supervisors *haven't* seen it all before.

In a gerontological setting, the presence of a student allows for the possibility of a new service. A social work student in a senior center may develop a group service for frail participants which enables them to better integrate into mainstream activities. A research study of patients discharged from a hospital with home care may measure effectiveness of home based services. These and other interventions often happen only because of the student presence in an agency, and in many ways change the course of gerontological social work practice. Unfortunately, few agencies offer the long-term services of a professional worker to the elderly and their families. Of this small group, even fewer document their interventions. The student experience with the elderly offers an arena for new ideas to be tested, and an opportunity to generate more advanced clinical thinking.

ASSIGNMENT SELECTION

In developing a student assignment, the supervisor considers the educational needs of the student as well as the service needs of the agency. In addition, the supervisor can look toward designing an assignment which may challenge existing assumptions or augment the literature in gerontological social work.

The field instructor is accountable to her agency to provide the best possible service to the client group. When she agrees to become a field instructor, she also becomes accountable to the school and to the student to provide a valid learning experience.

Ideally, the assignment exposes the student to a wide range of elderly clients, needs, and interventive modalities. This would include the young-old and the old-old, the able and the frail, men and women, couples and families, in the community, and in institutions, faced with developmental crises and situational crises. This varied population would be amenable to short- and long-term interventions either individually or in groups.

In reality, the extent of exposure is limited by the kind of population the agency serves, as well as the type of client the agency staff sees as needing help. Frail, very old widows who have difficulty adapting to institutional living will predominate in referrals for student assignments in a nursing home setting. Isolated and disabled elders may similarly predominate in the community. Group services are rare in community agencies where home visits are the norm. Service to families may be nonreimbursable and not offered on a routine basis either in the community or institution.

Moreover, agency service needs usually encompass a range of administrative tasks—compliance with government and board directives, recordings, etc.—beyond interaction with the client group. The agency standards for performance relate to what the staff member accomplished for the client within a specified time.

Educational expectations have a very different emphasis. There is still the demand to meet administrative requirements. However, satisfaction in an assignment relates to the process of the work and what the student learns.

The initial task for the field instructor, then, is to assess agency and educational needs and negotiate for assignments amenable to both parties. The field instructor assesses the agency and her own job objectively, thinking as an educator, as well as a professional employee. Answers to the following very basic questions provide guidelines:

What was my previous experience with students?

What assignments met the students' learning needs and had meaning to the agency?

What assignments didn't work out? Why did they fail?

What could have improved a particular assignment?

What isn't being done that a student could initiate?

Students have been in this particular service for several years. It is still a good use of student time? Is the outcome productive?

What information do I have about this student, and how can I use it?

Answers to these questions are combined with thinking related to the particular needs of the arriving students:

Could this nursing staff handle a beginner with no experience with the elderly?

Has anyone initiated a program in this service before?

Has research ever been a part of this program?

Anne is an experienced field instructor who runs a community center for the aged. She anticipated the arrival of a young man beginning his first year of graduate social work training. Noting a musical performance background, she anticipated he would be comfortable participating in the large weekly socials. Since she ran an active planning group which organized these socials, she decided to give him this group as an assignment.

She felt that this active, optimistic group would provide him with an instant successful service, as well as free up her own time. Research about how well the center met the needs of the surrounding community interested her. However, she decided this was not an area to pursue with a beginner—at least until she had made an educational assessment of his abilities. Thinking of how to best utilize a male student, Anne considered assigning him to work as liaison to the local hospital to get more service for homeless men. However, she recognized her own tendency to focus more on the service needs of the client group than on the learning needs of the student. She decided on a more conservative course of some typical cases until she saw how well this particular student coped within the agency.

The student's learning needs are dependent on his year in school, chosen area of specialization, and personal interests. An initial assignment for a first-year student who enters graduate school directly from college with an interest in clinical practice differs from that of a second-year student with experience in a city agency who will return to an administrative role. Both will look different from the assignment for a Bachelor's-level student.

The field instructor knows that a young inexperienced student may take to the agency and the profession readily. Meanwhile, someone with preconceived notions may struggle all year to incorporate a broader view.

The assignment should be real and meaningful to the client, agency, and student. However, it should also be designed to offer the maximum amount of learning within the context of the particular agency.

First-year students in direct practice need basic knowledge and generic skills translatable to other populations and settings. This is especially important when the student is resistant to the aging population and disappointed in the placement. This is frequently the case with the first-year student who does not choose his field of practice.

The beginner's needs are best met through work with the mentally alert elderly who can communicate and work on problems. These students need to see the broad range of interventive possibilities with individuals and environments and gain experience as helping professionals. Beginners need validation through client growth or improvement. However, work with this population is more maintenance than change oriented. Thus, for beginners, individual, family, and group assignments are chosen primarily for generic properties, potential for success, and balance of concrete and counseling needs. If possible, inspirational properties—that challenge negative stereotypes about aging and mitigate many of the depressing aspects of the work—should also be included.

Second-year clinical students have different needs. The field experience must complement the curriculum and provide sufficient clinical complexity to challenge the more experienced learner. Assignments must reflect the need for specialized techniques—i.e., work with the cognitively and sensorially impaired, with aging families around caregiving and planning. These issues require a specialized knowledge base about the later years and the network of services for the aging.

SERVICE NEEDS – LEARNING NEEDS

First Year Case Examples

I. Mr. G., a 65-year-old chronic alcoholic, is a new admission to a nursing home. He is scapegoated by other residents and staff. The *service* need is to help Mr. G. adapt to a new living arrangement, monitor the alcoholism, and develop an individualized plan to meet his needs. The *learning* need is to understand the implications of alcoholism in the elderly, learn treatment interventions, and gain knowledge of group dynamics and the scapegoating process.

II. Mrs. L. is an 80-year-old, mildly-confused woman, whose daughters referred her to a community agency for help with placement. She wishes to maintain her own apartment and appears able to do this with appropriate supports. The *service* need is to develop a workable plan to maintain her safely and interpret her care needs to the family. The *learning* need is knowledge of the mentally frail, development of resources, and skill in work with the family unit.

III. A discussion group for recent retirees associated with a union. The *service* need is to provide a forum for retirees to adapt to a new lifestyle and obtain information about entitlements and resources. The *learning* need is an understanding of the skills of group work and the psycho-social issues surrounding retirement.

Second Year Case Examples

Second year cases are less typical and more complex. Cases which require greater depth of psycho-social understanding and gerontological knowledge should predominate.

I. Mr. and Mrs. R., a couple in their 80s, referred to a community agency. Mrs. R. is physically ill and confused. Mr. R. is attempting unsuccessfully to care for her but cannot tolerate help in the house. There is no close family. The *service* need is to develop a care plan for Mrs. R., and help Mr. R. accept her needs, and his own limitations, as well as mediate between the couple and the home help. The *learning* need is understanding and utilizing the underlying dynamics of the relationship along with mediation skills.

II. Mrs. Z., is the 70-year-old daughter of a nursing home patient, who monitors the medical care of her mother, and frequently disrupts the floor staff by demanding changes in treatment. The *service* need is helping Mrs. Z. understand her role in the institution and work with the staff. The *learning* need is in assessment of her interaction with her mother and developing intervention strategies with family and staff.

III. Developing a group service for caregivers of elderly homebound patients. The *service* need is providing a supportive environment for an underserved population. The *learning* need is in development of more finely tuned group skills involving developing a service, understanding resistance, and formulating a beginning.

It is rarely possible or even desirable to have a complete assignment developed by the time the student arrives. Most often, assignments are developed within the first six weeks as the student's interests and abilities surface during the preliminary educational assessment. Assignments are developed with the following considerations in mind.

What does the student need to know? When must he know it? Social work field education is designed to be primarily experiential. Students must sit face to face with a client within the first weeks of field placement. Moreover, social work students encompass a broad range of backgrounds. They may come to the profession directly from undergraduate education with no work experience. Or students may have several years in the social work field and have returned to school to gain the necessary credentials. They may also have substantial experience in a related field, or perhaps come from a completely unrelated background.

Evaluation criteria provided by the school indicates the minimal standards for acceptable practice. However, minimum criteria do not accurately reflect the differing abilities of a natural beginner or the struggle of a highly-experienced returnee to move beyond preconceived notions. Social work education, like social work practice, is based on an individualized assessment. The expectations for practice will vary depending on the student's background, experience, intellectual ability, and understanding of the field. Initially, the supervisor uses the information from the school, as well as the student's initial presentation, to begin the educational assessment. Of particular concern for the beginning assessment is how the individual learns best.

Different Types of Learners and Their Beginnings with Clients

The Intuitive Learner will be most comfortable getting "in there" with the client, and pulling out issues from the experience. The Intellectual Learner will need more theoretical knowledge before beginning. The Practical Learner will respond best to immediate, clear feedback and can most benefit from role play before the first encounter.

Mrs. K., an 89-year-old widow living alone with house-keeping assistance is referred to a community mental health center by her physician because she seems depressed and isolated. Each student would begin with her somewhat differently.

Joan, a first year student with a background in banking, is quick to involve herself at the agency and tends to need a real person to begin. Encouraged by the supervisor to go in and listen, she is comfortable asking Mrs. K. to talk about herself. She notes as much about Mrs. K. and her environment as possible. In reviewing the process recording with her supervisor, Joan can look at Mrs. K.'s description of her lifestyle and understand her difficulty coping with changes in her situation as her health declines.

Assigned to David, who entered social work school after completing a degree in philosophy, Mrs. K. would wait a little longer for service. She would meet her social worker after he learned enough about depression in the aged to assess the possibility of either a reactive or endogenous depression. Although David could not learn everything before the encounter, he would be more comfortable knowing that physical illness, poor nutrition, and social isolation are all common causes of depression-like symptoms in the elderly. The intellectual learner needs to place the person in context before engaging. With Mrs. K., he will ask questions designed to identify symptoms of depression. Eliminating clinical symptoms, David will look for socio-environmental factors as clues for work.

Margaret is a second-year student with a teaching background. She knows that supervision will help her to understand and help Mrs. K. As Mrs. K. in a role-play situation, she begins to imagine how Mrs. K. might feel. As herself again, she notes her supervisor's responses and concerns as Mrs. K.

None of these categories is, of course, absolute. The Intellectual Learner gets his questions from the experience. The Intuitive Learner must know enough about depression in the elderly to recognize symptoms. Practical learning uses a combination of experience and intellect. Thus, the supervisor who can assess how best the student learns will move the student more quickly down his educational path.

SUPERVISORY CONFERENCE

The student and the supervisor spend a lot of time together in individual conferences, as required by schools of social work. The general requirement is one to two hours weekly, depending on other educational opportunities offered in the agency. The supervisor does not lecture for that time. In fact, she should not lecture at all. Process recordings are usually the focus of supervisory sessions, but their use varies greatly. What *really* happens in supervision?

The core tension in supervision, at least in the beginning, is usually the supervisor's certainty that learning must come from the student, and the student's equal certainty that the supervisor can and must tell him what to do. Social work supervision is, for most beginning students, a learning experience unlike any they have known before. According to the educational model of classroom teaching, the instructor communicates information to the student, who demonstrates learning through exams and papers. The predominant supervision model is administrative. The worker is monitored to see that he performs his work in a timely, effective manner. In social work education, a student must record all details of an interview, including his opinions and feelings toward the client. He may be puzzled by the process: Is it psychotherapy? Why are answers being withheld when the supervisor obviously knows them?

This anxiety is compounded by the content to be taught. In most professions, the subject material is acknowledged as specialized and available only to those who have made a concentrated study of the area. It is possible to identify the moment when one has passed from not knowing to knowing how to conduct a cross-examination or fill a cavity. Social work skills are different. Their acquisition is a subtle process of blending professional values, knowledge, and skills with the individual character of the practitioner. It is this that is referred to as the professional use of self.

Because learning is gradual, uneven, and evident in some areas before others, it is difficult for the student to realize when it occurs.

Further, close supervisory attention is paid to his personal reactions to clients, and he may fear that his privacy is being invaded. Most important, he may feel that a judgment of his work is a judgment of his character.

The initial engaging and contracting with the student in supervision must address these concerns. The supervisor needs to clarify supervision with an explanation of content and process. To tell a first-semester student that learning must come from him is useless and anxiety provoking. A student may not even know what he should know or how to frame the questions in the beginning.

The description of social work skills, and how they can be learned in supervision, will offer the student both intellectual content and assurance that the supervisor can help.

> Beginning with a first-year student, the supervisor explained that they would begin engaging the client. She asked the student how she thought an elderly nursing home patient could be engaged. Isolated in a nursing home, they agreed that the patient might be happy to see anyone. On the other hand, the supervisor raised issues of physical impairments common to the elderly which can make communication more difficult than anticipated. She suggested talking clearly, repeating, and changing phrasing to ensure the client understands.

In the preceding example, the supervisor prefaces the discussion with identification of the skill that is to be learned: engagement. She then draws on the student's experience and common sense to develop professional skill. Finally, she offers the professional knowledge and gerontological expertise needed to help the student learn.

The supervisor must also be sensitive to the student's reactions to first experiences in the field. Work with the aging is often stressful to the student. Nevertheless, supervision is not therapy, and time spent on personal issues must be designated as such.

> The supervisor noted that Jane's eyes filled with tears as she recounted her interview with Mrs. Y. Jane said she was upset because Mrs. Y. reminded her of her late grandmother. The supervisor noted that Jane's reactions to clients were often per-

sonal. She wondered if that had to do with the elderly population. Jane said it did, and talked at length about how respect
for the old was insisted upon in her family. Often it was hard
for her to make demands on clients. She was aware, in fact,
that she would sometimes not raise issues if she thought her
client would get mad. She mentioned that this was not the case
with Mrs. Y. because her grandmother never was angry with
her. The supervisor suggested they take a five-minute break
from the work. She said she would like to know more about
Jane's grandmother and other people in her family if she
would like to tell her.

The supervisor was careful to preface this time-out discussion
with an explanation that personal experiences and feelings often get
in the way of the work. Identifying differences between one's own
family and the client group is necessary. Thus, Jane heard that her
whole life was not up for discussion. Her feelings about elders
would only be examined as they affected her practice. (See Appendix D for a process recording of a supervisory conference.)

The Conference Agenda

Both supervisor and supervisee should come to the conference
with an agenda. The student should submit his agenda in advance.
The agenda is a useful tool for the supervisor in understanding what
the student sees as a learning issue, and how he formulates areas of
interest and concern. In the beginning, agenda items are usually
practical (how to get a food stamp application), or globally complex
(Do the K.'s need marriage counseling and how should I begin?").
The supervisor needs to use the agenda items to respond to the
student's worries and to teach conceptual thinking. In helping the
student develop an agenda, the emphasis should be on what has
been learned and what is the obstacle to learning. The supervisor
should be alert to the student's struggles and help her to discuss
them. At the end of a conference, the supervisor can suggest items
for the next conference: "Think about what aspects of family work
are unclear to you, and we will focus on them next week." The
student then thinks of practice in a more specific way:

Agenda:

How to engage Mrs. M.'s son to plan with Mrs. M. when he responds "ask my sister."

How to encourage the sister to include her brother and give up some of her role as caretaker.

RECORDING

Agencies, schools, and individual field instructors often disagree on the type and quantity of recording most useful in educational supervision. Audio and video tape summary recording and process recording are used in various combinations.

Taping. When taping is possible it can be a useful teaching material, especially in developing self-awareness. The student can observe himself and the client at a distance—free of the anxiety of the interview situation. It can also be useful to the supervisor, revealing small but significant non-verbal and verbal interactions that might not be recorded in written form. Drawbacks to the use of tapes are financial (they may be costly), practical (they take more time to review than recordings), and legal (they require releases from clients). Moreover, they are inappropriate for many elders and settings.

Summary Recordings are useful for teaching students how to conceptualize and condense their observations. These skills are necessary for chart notes and other forms of recording required by agencies. Summary recordings can also keep supervisors apprised of developments in student cases that, for lack of time, cannot be process recorded each week.

Students often prefer to talk about their work either before or instead of writing about it. While the supervisor's immediate input may often be necessary for a timely intervention, habitual reliance on "talking about" robs the conference of much of its teaching potential.

Process Recording

As the focus of work, the process recording is crucial to the supervisory conference. However, it can be used differentially, depending on the student's learning needs. A student needing to work on empathizing and feeling with the client will frequently benefit from line-by-line review with a focus on recreating the experience.

Supervisor: "How did you feel when she said no?" "What did he look like then?"

A student needing to conceptualize issues from the individual experience can use the recording to develop ideas.

Supervisor: "Tell me about Mrs. A." "What is your assessment at this point?"

The student using the process recording for critical analysis benefits most from developing the ability to identify successful interventions and problems.

Student: "I thought I was really reading Mr. R. correctly, but at a certain point, I had trouble understanding what he was feeling. I'm not sure what went wrong here."

Supervisor: "Let's go back to the process to identify what was happening for you and for Mr. R."

It is not helpful to give back recording with comments to the student before supervision. The student may react defensively, try to explain away his problems, feel like a failure, or not develop his own ideas. Even positive comments are less than helpful because the student often does not know why an intervention was good or how he can repeat it. However, reviewing a process recording with comments *after* supervision can augment or reinforce some of the discussion.

Students often fear that they will not remember exactly what happened. However, verbatim replication is not the purpose of process recording. Rather, the student reproduces what he recalls as important even if he does not recognize or respond to its significance within the interview. The supervisor is then able to bring it into his awareness.

In Jenna's recording, Mr. P. kept repeating how well off he was compared to other older people. Jenna kept responding with a recitation of the services the agency could offer him. Her accurate rendering (if not understanding) of the communication problem opened the door to a productive supervisory discussion.

GROUP SUPERVISION

Group Projects

When there are several students placed at an agency, it is wise to think of some form of group supervision as an adjunct to individual supervision. Weekly meetings as a unit, with one field instructor as leader, can be structured many ways to serve many ends.

In the beginning of the year, the group meeting can be the vehicle for orientation to the agency and preparation for initial work with clients. Lectures on different aspects of the agency's work and follow-up written material are the easiest ways to do this. Unfortunately, this method can grow boring, and students retain little. Participatory exercises ensure enthusiasm and hasten the formation of group cohesiveness.

Students may be asked to keep logs during the first week of placement. They record all their impressions and questions and share them at the first meeting. They may be sent on teams with a list of questions to explore the neighborhood, senior center, or hospital unit. When they return, they may have information to contribute. This technique helps the field instructor ascertain their observational abilities and concerns. Explanations of the agency can then be tailored accordingly. Students may also participate in simulation exercises where they must accomplish simple tasks wearing blindfolds, wax in their ears, or be in a wheelchair. Many find such experiences helpful in beginning to empathize with aged clients whose world view is so different from their own.

The field instructor might also experiment with an exercise on listening and responding to typical responses of elderly clients at first meetings with their social worker. (Appendix C is a sample developed for a group of students beginning work at a nursing home.) One student can be asked to play the aged client, another his worker. The student-client can then be asked how he feels when he is the recipient of each student-worker response. Students have fun with this approach. It calls on their dramatic abilities and fosters camaraderie.

After the first month when students are well into the work, it is possible to shift to a practice conference format. This method can be related to a specific issue or focus on the practice of one student each week. An issue-related conference will require brief presentations by each student around one common problem such as communicating with medical personnel. A conference devoted to the work of one student will emphasize the importance of collaborative thinking on a work in progress rather than a judgement of performance. It will also give practice for case presentations of a more formal nature. In both cases, the field instructor will foster group discussion and mutual aid. She summarizes by underscoring general practice principles to be drawn from the examples.

A unit meeting early in the semester focused on how to obtain and utilize medical information. The supervisor offered and encouraged some ventilation of feelings about the physicians. She acknowledged that dismissive responses are not uncommon. Use of role play helped the students identify some reasons for the physician's responses. Students also were able to begin to identify points of common interest and work on how to present effectively. Each had an opportunity to act as the social worker and get feedback from the others. The supervisor helped them identify skills needed to engage different professionals, and how to focus the conversation to maximize the informative sharing. Since several students worked with doctors with foreign training, she took the opportunity to comment on socio-cultural differences, as well as differences in professional training.

At a later meeting, one student presented the case of Mrs. L., a mildly confused, 85-year-old lady who lived independently with a housekeeper. Her daughter sought help with nursing home placement, as she worried about her gradual decline. The student's initial assessment was that Mrs. L. could manage at home at present. At the unit meeting, the supervisor focused on how to intervene to help the family work together. Initial tendencies of the students' to advocate for Mrs. L. were discussed. Role play helped the students to understand the daughter's viewpoint. The group was comfortable with mediating in the situation. Emphasis on understanding the problems, but not feeling the need to solve problems for the clients, was reinforced in the group.

The group also provides the students with an experiential learning situation in developing group skills. As a group member, the student sees himself and his peers act out group dynamics in a real-life situation. He also sees the field instructor modelling the group leader he will become.

By mid-year, it is useful to spend at least half of group supervision time on a group project. The project provides students with a rewarding hands-on experience in practice research or organizational change. They learn to work together in making a lasting contribution to the agency or to the field. In the process, they discover the rewards and frustrations of such efforts.

The genesis of a project can come from many sources and fan out in many directions. We list some of the projects that our student units have accomplished as examples of what might be done.

The Day Care Expansion Project

The director of a Day Care Program had funds to expand the program to more participants but questioned its feasibility. The students were enlisted to work together on a needs assessment of the community. Using the supervisor as a consultant, they each explored different sources of information. They approached the community agencies, planning boards and the Borough President's office to obtain demographic and service data. They were encouraged to consider new approaches in case finding, program planning, and agency policy. In this way, they integrated their class work with field experience. The final report recommended several changes in the program to precede expansion.

The Resident Council Project

A group of students were particularly interested in individual rights in the nursing home. They proposed to study the workings of the Resident Council, and its viability as an instrument of organizational change. They analyzed the bylaws of the council, interviewed staff and residents and tracked one complaint through the council system. This group raised significant issues about the council and made some useful recommendations for improvement.

Discharge from Short-Term Rehabilitation

Students developed a questionnaire for a follow-up study of elders in the community who had been discharged from the short-term rehabilitation unit of a hospital within the past year. The findings of this study were instrumental in obtaining a grant to extend social work services beyond the point of discharge.

Loss and Bereavement

A unit of clinically-oriented students decided to study the opportunity to mourn the death of peers within a nursing home. The interests of one administrative student expanded the project into an in-depth study of how the various disciplines function when a resident dies. The result: recommendations of changes in the role of each department. The report had a major impact on the agency which developed an interdisciplinary team to implement most of the recommendations.

Students often respond to the initial idea of a project hesitantly and fearfully. They may see little relevance to their clinical concerns. It sounds very hard and feels like a lot of extra work. However, the unit project provides an opportunity for creativity and initiative that is not available in any other assignment. While the supervisor is crucial in providing guidance and mediating disagreements, the group is responsible for task accomplishment. Students soon understand that the project will be as in-depth as they decide.

They learn to use time productively and effectively. As the supervisor helps the group break down the project into manageable pieces, she is modelling the skill of partialization. As students develop tools to gather information and implement ideas, they also begin to identify individual interests and strengths. The field instructor soon sees areas of strength in some students that were not apparent in the individual work. As the group progresses the interplay among the members becomes more dynamic and the students live the group experience. The supervisor moves in and out of the group. She is always available but able to stand back and let the group develop on its own. At the end of the project, the group has learned about clinical interventions, organization, research, group process, and systems. This learning experience can lead to long lasting organizational change. Each student has also developed many skills.

EVALUATION

Evaluation of a student is an ongoing process that begins at the first meeting between student and supervisor. It should always be a shared process. The supervisor is responsible for keeping the student apprised of his progress in learning. The student should never be surprised to find he is doing exceptionally well or exceptionally poorly. He should not even be surprised during the mid-semester evaluation, as the supervisor's reactions to his work should be shared on an ongoing basis. Students should be assisted in identifying helpful interventions and conceptualizing theory from practice.

At first, the student will not have the ability to judge his own work. He may only know what felt right and what went wrong. However, slowly, and with great individual variation, he should be able to identify his own practice strengths and problems related to professional criteria.

Mid-Semester Evaluation

A written assessment early in the semester is helpful to the supervisor in clarifying her thinking. Such an evaluation also gives the student documentation to refer to. A written Educational Assessment and Plan is an excellent follow-up to the Mid-Semester Oral

Evaluation. Most schools of social work suggest that the Mid-Semester Oral Evaluation be conducted six weeks into the first and third semester. While not the detailed evaluation required at the end of each term, this preliminary summary provides the framework for future supervisory conferences. It also gives the student a precise picture of his initial status as a student.

Sometimes, supervisors experience situations where the student has difficulty identifying practice strengths and weaknesses and cannot hear the supervisor's intervention. The student is not lying but truly has not heard discussion of his level of practice. The written document is an important tool in such situations.

Six-Week Educational Assessment and Plan

Ellen Johnson Clinical Practice
Second Year November 1988

Ms. Johnson comes to the Hatfield Nursing Home with an interest in aging and a strong motivation to learn social work skills with the elderly. Her first-year field placement was with troubled adolescents and she has some work experience in a medical setting. Ms. Johnson is a dedicated, committed person who easily involved herself in the agency and with the population. She is empathic in her approach and communicates well. However, she needs more clarity about her role as a helping professional. Ms. Johnson is quick to offer solutions, and needs to concentrate during this semester on developing skills in exploration and reaching for underlying feelings. Her capacity to assess environmental obstacles and strengths is well-developed. In strengthening assessment skills, the focus will be on intrapsychic obstacles. Ms. Johnson is strong in identifying and engaging services and resources. She also displays a well-developed knowledge of the agency and staff. Although responsive in supervision, she is most comfortable in the student role and is hesitant to offer her own opinions and ideas. Goals for the semester include: (1) Developing capacity to explore client need, (2) More psychodynamic assessments, (3) Staying with painful feelings of clients, (4) Taking more risks in the learning process. Ms. Johnson's assignments consist of four long-term cases and one small group (a Reminiscence Group on a skilled nursing unit). She will soon be assigned to telephone inquiry duty in the Intake Department to develop capacity in short-term assessment and intervention. Ms. Johnson has read and agrees with this evaluation and plan.

The mutual assessment process that leads to the six-week educational assessment and plan is a useful point of departure for discussion with the field advisor. Here, the supervisor has a concept of the student as a learner and practitioner. In addition, the early gains in practice skills and primary areas for further development have been spelled out and can be verbally shared with the advisor.

Semester Evaluation

When the semester draws to a close, the supervisor must provide the school with a written critique of the student's practice. Having gone through the process of evaluation with the student once during the mid-semester oral evaluation, it is generally easy to develop the approach to discussing practice. However, the demand to provide a detailed accounting to the school is often anxiety producing to both supervisor and student. No matter how much verbal feedback has been offered, the written evaluation represents a definitive representation of the student at a particular time.

For the supervisor, particularly a beginning supervisor, preparing the written evaluation often arouses latent feelings of inadequacy and insecurity: "Have I taught enough?" "Was I clear?" "Was I available enough?" "Should I have done more?" Similarly, the student may experience anxiety, a regression back to early school days when outcome was thought to depend on the teacher's approval. The wish to do well may thus supplant the ability to assess the work and level of development. Furthermore, a student who has returned to school after independent employment may have difficulty being a student and become defensive or dismissive of the evaluation process.

The supervisor will first need to handle her own anxiety. Focusing on the importance of her professional role will allow her to be more objective in her responses. Similarly, the supervisor helps alleviate the student's anxiety by structuring the evaluation process. The first stage is the provision of specific steps to prepare for the evaluation conference.

In planning the evaluation conference, the supervisor should ask the student to read the performance criteria for the semester and review all of her process recordings. The supervisor, of course, does the same. Process recordings may be read chronologically, a case at a time (if the work is long-term), or week by week (when crisis and short-term work prevails). The purpose of the reading is two-fold: to assess skills development in particular situations and over time.

Supervisor and student should enter the conference with specifics. These examples illustrate practice skills, growth in ability, or areas needing further development. The supervisor must hear the student out, demonstrating that evaluation is a mutual process. If the supervisor has already made up her mind, it will be evident to the student. At the same time, the supervisor is the professional with professional standards to uphold. She must give the student a fair hearing. She must not, however, let the student control the process, or tell her what should be included.

How can the supervisor hear out the student if she has already made a professional assessment? During the evaluation conference, the supervisor must carefully and thoroughly explore the student's comments and assessment of the work. Often the student's thinking does not differ much from the supervisor's assessment, but needs to be conceptualized as an issue for work.

Sally's supervisor asked how she saw herself developing as a group worker. Sally indicated that she loved groups, and felt her contracting and exploring was good. The supervisor asked what helped her. Sally talked about the receptivity of the members of the senior planning group and how much she liked them. The supervisor asked what was hard in beginning with groups. Sally talked about difficulty dealing with other staff and the obstacles to beginning a service. They agreed that Sally found negative reactions hard to deal with and agreed on it as an area for future work.

Despite the demand for review of the work and self-analysis, students may come to the evaluation conference unprepared or with vague, unfocussed self-observations: "I know I have a lot to learn" or "I finally think I know what social work is about." For the student to take responsibility for his learning, the supervisor must refuse to proceed until the student has done the requisite preparation. She should stick to this course, even if it means postponing the conference. The student's ability to take responsibility will vary depending on semester. However, the supervisor must always help the student understand the importance of the evaluation process by demanding preparation.

The actual writing of the evaluation is the supervisor's job. Demands on the student to do any more than review and discuss his own performance are inappropriate and unethical.

The written evaluation is often effectively looked at as progress over time.

> Elaine's discomfort with the setting and the population was evident in her beginning practice. She viewed the client group stereotypically making assumptions about "old people's" needs and wants. Attempts to stay with affectual content and explore concerns came across as insensitive and challenging rather then helpful. As Elaine became more familiar with the agency and responded to supervision, she began to see the population as individuals with particular problems and concerns. Her group was especially useful to her in developing a sense of what a social worker does to help. Her strengths emerged in the group. As she experienced members responding when she asked rather than told, she began to relax, and transfer skills developed in the group into the practice with individuals.

Another student's practice may be best understood in the context of patterns.

> Robert is not fully comfortable in the social work role. He has difficulty presenting himself as a professional. This situation makes his interventions uneven. Good beginning contracting is evident in his work. However, Robert moves away from

ambivalent reactions. His ongoing work follows the same pattern of uneven interventions. He responds sensitively to painful situations but moves away when the client responds negatively, or feels hopeless.

The evaluation need not be lengthy. However, it should be specific, and individualized, explicating one student's ability to practice social work.

Problem Students

Social workers become student supervisors for many reasons. It is gratifying to provide the atmosphere for learning, to teach skills, and to share one's practice wisdom. Assuming a nurturing supportive role with clients comes naturally to the gerontological social worker and is easily translated to the supervisory experience. At the same time, field instruction is often the first time that the social worker serves in an administrative role, occupying a position of sanctioned authority over others. The conflict between the two functions is nowhere more apparent than in the evaluation process.

When all goes well, evaluation is a mutually congratulatory experience that enhances the confidence of supervisor and supervisee. However, when the student's progress is not evident, it is much harder for the supervisor. It is difficult to criticize and make someone else unhappy. However, learning problems must be identified and openly discussed early. Supervisors may feel uncomfortable being open about the student's learning problems. However, they need to keep in mind how much more difficult identifying problems will be later in the semester. The possibility of resolving learning issues without arousing defensiveness is greater the earlier it occurs.

Schools of social work appoint faculty members who serve as liaisons to agency-based supervisors. It is their responsibility to work closely with the field instructor when a student is experiencing unusual difficulty. It is helpful to the struggling student to have the supervisor tell him that she is contacting the advisor. Academic workloads may be great and field advisors are not always in a position where they reach out to the supervisor. It is thus important and appropriate for the supervisor to reach out to the field advisor and ask for help. If such an encounter is unavailable or unsatisfactory, the school's department of field work should be contacted. As the agency supervisor has a responsibility to the school, so the school has a responsibility to the agency supervisor. Neither can educate the student to be an effective social work practitioner without the help of the other.

Chapter 7

Administrative Supervision

The nature of the social work service and the organization of staff is dependent on the particular agency. The size of the agency is most significant to gerontological social work supervisors. It affects the collegial relationships open to her and her workers. A large social work department facilitates advocating for client causes and worker rights. This potential is not present in a smaller setting. At the same time, the numbers lend themselves to bureaucratic difficulties.

The public setting or the setting largely funded by governmental programs typically has the most bureaucratic regulations. These situations also have the least opportunity for worker autonomy in task accomplishment.

A public agency will require the social worker to implement social policy through a variety of procedures and with extensive documentation. The worker can anticipate layers of bureaucracy, each with limited authority. Change is usually slow although directives from the top can change rapidly. Social work service is determined by fiscal regulations. Reimbursement for service to the elderly may not recognize the need to work with family members. Or policy may allow for only a certain number of visits in a fiscal year regardless of needs. It is difficult, though not impossible, to influence this system, as political considerations are usually primary motivations in establishing and implementing service.

Proprietary organizations reflect the capitalist system of our society. Nursing homes and home-care agencies more commonly exist for profit than other service agencies. The need to make a profit is primary, and service is geared in that direction. Often agencies directed to profit provide good service. However, for the social worker, providing a softer, less-easily measured service, ethical dilemmas can emerge quickly. As a supervisor, one must be alert to maintain professional standards of practice. Paraprofessional workers with little training are most frequently found in settings operated under proprietary auspices. In these cases, the supervisor is usually a consultant, hired on an hourly basis to fill mandated government requirements.

The private sector in gerontological social work is most often filled by Geriatric Care Managers in small (frequently one-person) operations. These managers charge on a fee-for-service basis.

Voluntary agencies are most compatible to the profession and gerontological practice. Although often governed by federal/state regulations and funded by public monies, a voluntary agency has an established mission to serve a target population. Policy can change or be modified through assessment of needs, as well as fiscal constraints or change in government regulation. An employee has access to a smaller chain of command. In many agencies, any employee has access to the Executive Director. Certainly, any supervisor in a voluntary agency has the means to promote improved service or a change in policy. Life is not easy or always rewarding in a voluntary agency. However, possibilities for providing better service in a more benevolent setting are much greater than in public or proprietary settings.

Resources available to gerontological social workers are tied to auspices and funding sources. The public sector often has the fewest, with social workers functioning in a sense like double agents. They balance client service and gate-keeping functions.

Variables of setting are as important as the training and experience of the worker in determining the role of the gerontological social work supervisor. The presence of abundant worker supports in collegial relationships may dictate use of group or peer supervision as an adjunct to, or substitute for, individual supervision. A single worker in a setting will need more opportunities for impromptu or phone contact with the supervisor. Such contacts buttress or reenforce professional identification.

An agency may dictate that workers limit services to needy elders. As a results, they may experience conflict. Such feelings must be addressed in settings where supervisory conferences may focus on a preponderance of ethical issues. The private practitioner who seeks supervision may have different ethical conflicts: whether her primary client is the adult child who pays the fee or the elderly parent. The large voluntary agency blessed in resources and collegiality may nevertheless precipitate problems with interdisciplinary collaboration. Thus, the supervisory assessment of specific strengths and deficits of the setting should be considered in the assessment of each worker's learning and practice needs.

Social work is unique among professions in the assumption that supervision continues past accreditation to practice. Although a graduate of social work school is a qualified social worker, he is only beginning a professional career. Good social work practice dictates two years of intensive, ongoing supervision. This time frame is also required for professional accreditation from the Academy of Certified Social Workers (ACSW) issued by the National Association of Social Workers. Is such extensive supervision necessary and productive for a full-fledged professional? Does it foster unhealthy dependency? Or is it a way of developing a mature, competent professional? In addition, are there any unusual aspects of gerontological social work that make supervision more helpful?

When a professional sees an atypical situation, consultation with a specialist is a natural response. While social work skills are learned and constant, social work interventions are always dissimilar because human beings are never exactly the same. Frequently, a particular skill translates from one situation to another, but each situation needs a careful and differential assessment. Ongoing supervision is significant in social work because of the need to think anew *how* skills are to be used in each case.

In addition, the supervisory relationship provides support, knowledge, and an opportunity for self-understanding. These factors can be instrumental in preventing social work burn out.

In gerontology, ongoing supervision is of particular importance. There is much expertise about the aging which must be learned on the job. Students completing social work school seldom have had formal course work in the field. They often possess only a superficial understanding of the problems facing the aged or of the range of possible interventions. Moreover, the problems of the aged have so many dimensions that the beginning worker needs supervisory assistance to partialize and prioritize what must be done.

Often the overwhelmed or irritated worker is not responding to job pressures at all. Rather she may lack the necessary clinical skills to meet client needs.

> Joan is a worker with two years of post-Master's experience in an adult residence. She complained bitterly about the time speaking to families took away from her work with residents. She particularly resented the demands of one "manipulative" daughter who was detaining her with complaints about service. The supervisor recognized that while Joan was effective with residents and staff, she needed more knowledge and skills to deal with family members.

Sometimes, workers think they are in the midst of ethical dilemmas when they actually lack clinical skills. While there *are* true ethical dilemmas, they are fewer than may appear to the inexperienced worker.

> Peter wanted to consult the ethicist recently employed by his hospital for help in this case. The problem was that the husband insisted his wife not be told of her diagnosis, and the wife was repeatedly asking what was wrong with her. The supervisor reframed the problem as a practice issue: how to explore with the husband his fears about his wife's response, and how to facilitate communication within the marriage.

Supervision of even an inexperienced worker is very different from supervision of students. The focus and purpose of the relationship are not the same. In supervision of a student, the focus is on the learning. What knowledge and skills did the student gain from the experience? In administrative supervision, while education is always important, the focus is more on the outcome. How did the worker's intervention help the client.

Administrative supervision addresses the use of agency resources (including the skills of its workers). How can these resources best be allocated? In educational supervision, the variety and frequency of interventions will be determined by assessing the client's service needs and the student's learning needs. In administrative supervision, the client service need may be secondary to the resources available and to the needs of other clients. The worker's professional growth may be disregarded altogether.

A beginning supervisory issue in administrative supervision is establishing priorities and parameters of service.

Nancy is a June graduate beginning in a small community agency. She anticipated an afternoon getting to know Mrs. L., who received homemaking and transportation services from the agency. In planning her initial contact, she was surprised when her supervisor suggested she limit her home visit to half an hour. They discussed Mrs. L.'s current needs. The supervisor agreed that an in-depth understanding of Mrs. L. would be useful. She also pointed out that Mrs. L. had been stable. She encouraged Nancy to save in-depth assessments for newer cases and emergencies.

Administrative supervision is much more dependent on verbal reporting of the worker than on written material. Process recording is neither feasible nor appropriate for administrative supervision. Supervision should concentrate on certain areas—new cases, highly complex situations, or problems involving agency systems. However, aside from those situations, issues raised depend largely on what the worker perceives as an issue or concern. The supervisor thus needs to be alert to what is and is not raised by the worker.

Andrew's supervisor noted that supervisory sessions over the past several weeks had consisted of a series of questions about tasks and issues related to forms. When questioned, Andrew said that the job required a lot of detail. When the supervisor pressed about some of the more clinically oriented situations, he became defensive. When the supervisor suggested he was feeling overwhelmed, he quieted down and agreed he was upset and exhausted.

The function of the administrative supervisor is parallel to that of the educational supervisor. A differential assessment of the supervisee is the key to a productive relationship. Even though there is less teaching with a professional worker, the supervision is similar. The supervisor starts with worker concerns and builds upon them. The primary purpose of administrative supervision is accountability for delivery of agency service. The supervisor directs the worker in the use of time and assessment of needs.

A student caseload is balanced to provide a variety of learning experiences. A worker's caseload is developed by catchment area, service unit, or other agency classification unrelated to the client's needs and problems. While a student often reaches out to provide service, a worker's attention will more likely be reactive to the most problematic and demanding cases. In these cases, he can be conflicted about how to intervene with demanding clients.

> Anne, a social worker at a rehabilitation center, brought a question about Mrs. C. to supervision. As they resolved it, the supervisor saw a flicker of concern on Anne's face. Questioned, Anne expressed resentment and anger at Mrs. C.'s unending demands. She also explained that limit setting didn't work because refusing to see her made the doctors and nurses (who were also having problems with Mrs. C.) angry. "No way out?" said her supervisor. Anne laughed. They discussed Mrs. C. and developed a sense of why she was so demanding and untrusting. The supervisor suggested that Mrs. C. sensed Anne's exasperation and dislike. She also suggested that shorter regular appointments might lessen the client's demanding behavior and Anne's distaste. They talked about staff reactions and worked on interpreting Mrs. C.'s behavior and engaging other staff to promote a consistent care plan.

The beginning worker will need help learning a different use of supervision in the worker role. As a student, she brought everything to supervision. As a worker, she must learn to make choices. When and how to act independently are thus issues for the beginning worker.

> Wendy had been an excellent student. She was committed to the profession and to her work. She was thorough in her assessments and explored every possibility before determining a course of intervention. In her first job, she continued to func-

tion the same way and put in hours of overtime. Her supervisor was frequently overwhelmed by the amount of supervision time Wendy needed. She discussed these issues with Wendy, including how to prioritize. Coming to grips with using assessments skills to prioritize was a struggle for Wendy and the focus of future work.

CONSULTATION

At the other end of the scale is the issue of the highly experienced worker. Since the purpose of administrative supervision is accountability, ongoing supervision is necessary. However, the time for independent practice has to come at some point in a practitioner's career. The supervisor and the worker set a goal for the time when supervision can become consultation. It is rare that the same supervisor and worker begin and arrive at the point of independence together. However, the ongoing evaluation of practice moves toward this goal. A senior worker keep the supervisor apprised of cases and problems. The worker will also bring unusual problems to the supervisor to discuss and determine strategy.

> Joanne, a long-time agency employee who also had a part-time private practice, brought Mr. K.'s current problems for discussion with her supervisor. She said that maybe she knew Mr. K. too well, as she kept getting lost in his complaints about his son. They discussed some of her past and current interventions with Mr. K. As Joanne talked, she realized that she was too identified with Mr. K. and was taking on his feelings about his son. She decided on a plan to bring Mr. K. and his son together for an open discussion.

Even the most experienced social worker needs a forum to talk through some of the overwhelming problems she confronts daily. Overidentification with an appealing client, anger at a demanding one, or frustration at an unresponsive system are all common human reactions. The supervisor can be 20 years younger with half the experience of the senior worker. She will still be helpful if she understands her role. She provides an arena to discuss, identify, and resolve problems interfering with the worker's practice.

RECORDING

Recording for the professional worker is an agency requirement rather than a supervisory one. The particulars of recording depend on agency needs and outside funding requirements. The supervisor should monitor recording for promptness and appropriate content. It is not uncommon for the worker to make recording low priority. Paperwork seldom feels significant in the helping process. The supervisor must believe, and make the demand, that timely recording can and must be a priority.

Recording provides the agency with documentation of its services. It also affords other staff understanding of the client's needs and the worker's interventions and plan.

The ability to do summary recording or a chart note is difficult for many workers to achieve. It requires a level of conceptualization and synthesis different from that needed to record recollections of an interview in process. It is useful for the supervisor to have models or outlines to be followed.

> Mrs. L.'s situation is currently stable. She continues to receive assistance from a home attendant who also does shopping and cooking. She appears increasingly anxious about her son's job transfer even though he will not be relocating. Continued exploration has not revealed any reason for heightened anxiety. Plan is to interview Mrs. L. with her son to further explore his transfer and her concerns. Psychiatric consult if anxiety reaction continues.
>
> Jane Willis, CSW

> During this period, 99-year-old, wheelchair-bound Mrs. O., whose diagnoses include dementia, osteoarthritis, functional paraparesis, s/p MI and cataracts, remained medically stable. At a 1/11/88 team meeting, she was noted to be unable to walk due to contractures and was at risk for skin breakdown. As a result of her dementia, she can be verbally disrup-

tive, screaming at other residents and agitated at times. She is treated with Hadol for this condition. In general, Mrs. O. can be observed sitting in her wheelchair, obviously disoriented and often appearing detached from her environment. She has the tendency to mumble to herself, sometimes calling out, but her speech is usually hard to understand. As a result, verbal communication with Mrs. O. is difficult. Mrs. O.'s brother is in frequent contact with me, usually concerning concrete service issues, but on occasion benefits from brief supportive counselling. He is a frequent visitor to his sister and a reliable family member. RCP: Show interest and support to Mrs. O. through brief individual contacts. Remain available to Mr. O. for assistance with concrete services or counselling as needed. Continue to monitor Mrs. O's overall functioning with interdisciplinary team. As previously noted, discharge planning is not possible. To be reviewed in six months.

Timothy Lerner, CSW

STAFF MEETINGS/PRACTICE CONFERENCES

The conference is not, of course, the only opportunity for learning available in most agencies. The supervisor must determine what issues should be handled in supervisory conference versus issues for staff meetings or practice conferences.

Use of staff meetings and the availability of practice conferences varies from agency to agency. However, even a small department is likely to have a staff meeting. Information is shared at staff meetings and discussion should also include administrative issues of general concern. Assessing Mr. K.'s need for escort service to a physician is an issue for the supervisory conference. The need for escorts in the population in general belongs in a staff meeting.

Service problems are abundant. However, the supervisor must also ensure that worker's complaints are not masking practice problems.

The supervisor explored a series of complaints about the services available for Mrs. M. The supervisor was aware that the worker's complaints were similar to Mrs. M.'s complaints to the worker. Confronted with this situation, the worker was able to see that she was projecting her own anger at the client onto the agency.

In an agency that uses practice conferences, this kind of example could be used as the focal point of discussion of a common practice problem. If the worker is helped to see that her response is understandable and not a personal failure, it can benefit her and other workers struggling with the same frustrations. A practice conference can also focus on a successful case. Examining good work reenforces practice strengths and identification of practice skills that may be used elsewhere.

Supervisors must look for a balance of case presentations. They must reach out for workers' ideas and identify practice problems of the staff for general discussion. The practice conference should always contribute to the learning process. If the supervisor has her own caseload, it can be useful for the supervisor to present a case to role model how to present. Workers will be able to see that practice struggles continue as a part of professional life.

Larger agencies often offer the opportunity for more advanced learning. A large social service department may have a speaker address a significant issue. Such a department may also allow workers to advance their knowledge in other areas by participating in interdisciplinary learning situations. A supportive supervisory relationship will encourage a reasonable amount of participation in larger learning opportunities. Workers have an ongoing struggle between meeting the clients' needs and advancing their own learning. One cannot participate in everything but should feel comfortable setting aside time for professional growth. A hospital or larger nursing home might, for example, have Grand Rounds organized to include interdisciplinary discussion. Community agencies can invite a professional to address issues of concern for staff.

Similarly, regular opportunities to participate in learning situations, such as conferences and continuing education workshops, outside the agency should be encouraged. Workers need to learn of new developments in their field and advance professionally. They also need to interact with other social workers beyond the confines of their own agencies. Opportunities for growth and learning keep morale high and provide the agency with higher quality personnel.

Employee Evaluation

While the student evaluation process is in many ways the culmination of an experience, worker evaluations are part of working life. A written professional evaluation for each social worker on a yearly basis is the ideal. However, few agencies can afford to meet this standard. Many agencies have a check-off evaluation for all employees. Any form that has room for comments can be adapted for a professional evaluation.

With an employee, evaluation is continuous. Supervision should provide feedback for the worker. The supervisor needs to identify strengths as well as focus on problem areas in supervision.

As with students, neither positive nor negative comments in evaluation should come as a surprise. They should be part of mutual process. Content areas are similar to the student evaluation, but the focus is different. Clinical capacity is always important. However, an employee evaluation must also address administrative demands. The ability to provide service to an entire caseload is as important as the clinical intervention in each case. The ability to shift priorities quickly is also very important.

Since the employee evaluation is not a final product, it is important that supervisor and supervisee have specific goals for the future. The worker's practice should be examined in an organized fashion. The evaluation should provide the framework for the working relationship.

Ex.	Employee evaluation
Christine Thomas	Employed 11/20/88
	Evaluation 11/1/89

Ms. Thomas was employed as a social worker in November of last year. This is her first social work position, though she has had experience as a teaching assistant. She came to the agency highly motivated to provide service to the elderly. Ms. Thomas has good beginning social work skills. She involved herself easily with the client group, responds sensitively to their needs, and has displayed good assessment skills in her psycho-social reports. Her field placements were in mental health agencies. Provision of concrete services is a new experience for her. She is often frustrated with an unresponsive system and appears unable to mobilize resources without supervisory direction. This is an area of continued work. Ms. Thomas is a friendly, outgoing young woman who enjoys good relationships with her colleagues. However, difficulties with less responsive staff members are also evident, and a pattern of intervention problems in difficult systems has emerged.

Ms. Thomas is a reliable employee who is on time and completes required recording and statistics in a timely manner. She is active in staff meetings and volunteered to present at a staff seminar during the year.

She is an overall highly-satisfactory employee. Goals for the coming year are:

1. learn eligibility requirements for medicaid, SSI, and other entitlements for elderly;
2. develop skills in negotiated systems;
3. develop alternatives when frustrated by unresponsive resources;
4. examine relationships in the agency, and develop more effective interventions.

ADMINISTRATIVE SUPERVISOR AS MIDDLE MANAGEMENT

Direct supervision is only one of the supervisor's roles. The supervisor is also accountable to upper management for the worker's performance. Feedback from other staff is always useful in assessing worker practice. However, the supervisor is in the best position to determine how the worker is practicing. She needs to put the feedback from other disciplines into context.

The agency administrator always praised Mark for his work and value to the agency. The supervisor was aware of Mark's fine clinical skills but also of his tendency to ingratiate himself with authority. She communicated the positive feedback and discussed authority issues with Mark.

Other situations require that the supervisor define the social work role and method. For example, non-social work staff in congregate settings often expect the social worker to solve difficult psychosocial problems on the spot. The supervisor's description of social work practice helps staff understand that the worker cannot perform magic and generates more realistic expectations. This advocacy effort of the supervisor also helps the worker feel validated and supported.

All supervisory intervention models practice. The impact of the supervisor on the system will have a trickle down effect on the workers. If good at the job, the supervisor's use of self will be reflected in the good practice of her supervisees.

As a middle-management employee, the supervisor is in a unique position. She is close enough to the hands-on experience to understand the clients' needs. She also has enough exposure to the administrative issues to understand larger needs or limitations.

Organizational change requires skill in influencing the key policymakers in an agency. Although any good social worker will easily identify many unmet needs, resources are limited. Every agency chooses to serve one category of need, while another equally deserving area is not addressed. As an initial step, the supervisor assesses the feasibility of change.

A supervisor at a YMCA Senior Center noted the workers' concerns about the frail elderly who could no longer come in for programs. She decided to develop a program to present to administration. In her plan, one of the social workers would move into a housing complex for the elderly one afternoon a week for social programs. She also contacted an agency that provided in-home counseling of the elderly. She worked out a direct referral system for clients who needed individual counseling.

In this example, the supervisor broadened the agency's scope by providing the same service in a different site. This solution is a relatively simple, inexpensive way of offering service to more people who need it. The supervisor also worked out a mechanism to provide the individual counseling through another agency.

The social work profession works with people with problems. This is always an emotional experience for the worker. The administrative social work supervisor must appreciate these feelings, but also provide understanding of the larger system. An elderly client at risk in the community, with no family or friends, may have to move to the top of a waiting list of a community service agency. The supervisor must intervene to accomplish this goal. On the other hand, a Christmas dinner for participants in a day-care program is a fine idea. However, it may not be possible in a small agency because of cost or need for sanitary kitchen facilities. The supervisor's role in this instance is to interpret the obstacles to the workers and help them look for outside resources.

Organizational change considers the importance of the issue, the resources available, and the possibility of successful outcome. Opportunities to empower the client population are also important to address, as long as the supervisor recognizes the need for all parties to participate in the process.

> The senior center administrator regretfully announced that he must cut back the lunch program. All participants in the center were upset. At spontaneous meetings, elders suggested petitions and calling the press as strategies to counteract the plan. The social worker, being identified primarily with the clients, perceived the cut back as indication of the administrator's lack of caring.
>
> The supervisor, understanding the current budget difficulties and seeing the potential for enormous problems, worked to defuse the situation. She suggested that the social worker help the members determine a course of action in addition to petitions. She alerted the administrator of the participants' anger and the possibility of a petition. She reminded him that social action was psychologically beneficial for the participants although she agreed it was hard "on us." She encour-

aged and supported the social worker. However she also reminded her the problem might not be resolved in the clients' favor. As the social worker began to see the issue as a process, she was able to work more productively with the group. At the same time the supervisor continued discussion with the administrator. In so doing, the supervisor computed the cost of lunch and persuaded the administrator to present a plan which would allow for lunch at a small fee. The social worker, meanwhile, primed the group for a negotiated settlement. At a large meeting, the administrator's plan was greeted with applause and cheers.

The issue in this example is a conflict between the perspective of workers allied with their clients and administrative decisions that appear to be in conflict with client well-being. It is the most common kind of problem the supervisor encounters. The supervisor must think through the range of possible interventions as well as their consequences. She thus speaks for the client while accommodating the administrative needs. Helping the social worker to mediate rather than advocate is primary, as is engaging the administrator in understanding clients' needs for control.

Administrative supervision is a difficult, but challenging and sometimes exhilarating function. Every aspect of the role provides opportunity for growth and learning for both the supervisor and her supervisees.

APPENDIXES

Appendix A

Selected Bibliography:
Social Work Supervision

Austin, Michael J. "Supervisory Management for the Human Services." Englewood Cliffs, NJ: Prentice Hall, 1981.

Berengarten, Sidney. "Identifying Learning Patterns of Individual Students: An Exploratory Study," *Social Service Review*, Vol. 31, No. 4, December 1975.

Bruner, Jerome S. *Toward a Theory of Instruction*. New York: W.W. Norton & Co., Inc., 1966.

Flapan, Dorothy. "Student Cotherapists as Facilitators for Group Patients," *Group, The Journal of the Eastern Group Psychotherapy Society*, Vol. 5, No. 3, Fall 1981.

Getzel, George, Goldberg, Jack and Salmon, Robert. "Supervising in Groups as a Model for Today," *Social Casework*, Vol. 52, March 1971.

Gitterman, Alex and Gitterman, Naomi Pines. "Social Work Student Evaluation: Format and Content," *Council on Social Work Education*, Fall 1979.

Gitterman, Alex and Miller, Irving. "Supervisors as Educators," *Supervision, Consultation and Staff Training in the Helping Professions*. Ed. Florence Kaslow. San Francisco: Josey Bass, 1977.

Golden, Kenneth M. "Client Transfers and Student Social Workers," *Social Work*, Vol. 21, No. 1, January 1976.

Gould, Robert Paul. "Student Experience with the Termination Phase of Individual Treatment," *Smith College Studies*, June 1978.

Halloway, S. Brager, G. *Supervising in the Home Services: The Politics of Practice*. New York: The Free Press, 1989.

Hawthorne, Lillian. "Games Supervisors Play," *Social Work*, Vol. 20, No. 3, May 1975.

Kadushin, Alfred. "Games People Play in Supervision," *Social Work*, Vol. 13, No. 3, March 1968.

————— *Supervision in Social Work*. New York: Columbia University Press, 1976.

Kahn, Eva. "The Parallel Process in Social Work Treatment and Supervision," *Social Casework*, November 1979.

Kaslow, Florence et al. *Supervision, Consultation and Staff Training in the Helping Professions*. San Francisco: Jossey-Bass, Inc., 1977.

Knowles, Malcolm. "Innovations in Teaching Styles and Approaches Based Upon Adult Learning," *Journal of Education for Social Work*, Vol. 8, No. 2, Spring. 1972.

Matorin, Susan. "Dimensions of Student Supervision: A Point of View," *Social Casework*, February 1979.

Middleman, Ruth R. and Rhodes, Gary B. *Competent Supervision*. Englewood Cliffs, NJ: Prentice-Hall, Inc., 1985.

Munson, Carlton E. *An Introduction to Clinical Social Work Supervision*. New York: The Haworth Press, 1983.

—————. *Social Work Supervision: Classic Statements, Critical Issues*. New York: The Free Press, 1979.

—————. "Style and Structure in Supervision," *Journal of Education for Social Work*, Vol. 7, No. 1, Winter 1981.

Perlman, Helen Harris, ". . . And Gladly Teach," *Journal of Education for Social Work*, Vol. 3, No. 1, Spring 1967.

Rehr, Helen and Caroff, Phyllis. *A New Model in Academic Practice Partnership; Multi-Instructor and Institutional Collaboration, in Social Work*. Lexington, MA: Ginn Press, 1986.

Reynolds, Bertha. *Learning and Teaching in the Practice of Social Work*. New York: Russell & Russell, NASW Classics Series, 1985.

Rosenblatt, Aaron and Mayer, John E. "Objectionable Supervisory Styles: Students' Views," *Social Work*, Vol. 20, No. 3, May 1975.

Rubin, Gerald. "Termination of Casework: The Student, Client and Field Instructor," *Journal of Education for Social Work*, Vol. 4, No. 2, Spring 1978.

Shulman, Lawrence. *Skills of Supervision and Staff Management*. Itasca, Illinois: F.E. Peacock Publishers, Inc., 1982.

Towle, Charlotte. *The Learner in Education for the Professions*. Chicago: University of Chicago Press, 1954.

Urdang, Esther. "In Defense of Process Recordings," *Smith College Studies in Social Work*, Vol. 50, No. 1, November 1979.

Watson, Kenneth. "Differential Supervision," *Social Work*, Vol. 18, No. 6, November 1973.

Webb, Nancy B. "From Social Work Practice to Teaching the Practice of Social Work," *Journal of Education for Social Work*, Fall 1984.

Wilson, Suanna. *Field Instruction Techniques for Supervisors*. New York: The Free Press, Inc., 1981.

Appendix B

Selected Bibliography: Gerontological Social Work Practice

Abramson, Julie S. "Participation for Elderly Patients in Discharge Planning: Is Self Determination a Reality?" *Social Work*, Vol. 33, No. 5, 1988.

Atchley, R. "A Continuity Theory of Normal Aging," *The Gerontologist*, Vol. 29, No. 2, April 1989.

Becket, Joyce, and Coley, Soroya M. "Ecological Intervention with the Elderly: A Case Example," *Journal of Gerontological Social Work*, Vol. 11, No. 1, 2, 1987.

Binstock, R. and George L. *Handbook of Aging and the Social Sciences* (3rd Edition). San Diego: Academic Press, Harcourt Brace Jovanovich, 1990.

Birren, J. and Schaie, K. *Handbook of the Psychology of Aging* (3rd Edition). San Diego: Academic Press, Harcourt Brace Jovanovich, 1990.

Brink, T.L. (Ed). *Clinical Gerontology: A Guide to Assessment and Interventions*. New York: The Haworth Press, 1985.

Brody, E. "Parent Care as a Normative Family Stress." Donald P. Kent Memorial Lecture presented at the 37th Annual Scientific Meeting of the Gerontological Society of America. San Antonio, Texas, 1954.

Brody, E. *Long Term Care of Older People: A Practical Guide*. New York: Human Sciences Press, 1977.

Burack-Weiss, A. "Clinical Aspects of Case Management," *Generations*, Fall 1988.

Busse, E. and Blazer, D. *Handbook of Geriatric Psychiatry*. New York: Van Nostrand Reinhold, 1980.

Butler, R. and Lewis, M. *Aging and Mental Health*. St. Louis, Missouri: C.V. Mosby Co., 1983.

Butler, R. *Why Survive: Growing Old in America*. New York: Harper & Row, 1975.

Callagher, Dolores and Thompson, Larry W. et al. *Depression in the Elderly: A Behavior Treatment Manual*. The Ethel Percy Andrus Gerontology Center, 1981.

Edelson, Jacqueline Singer and Lyons, Walter H. *Institutional Care of the Mentally Impaired Elderly*. New York: Van Nostrand Reinhold Co., 1985.

Edenberg, Mark A. *Mental Health Practice with the Elderly*. New Jersey: Prentice Hall, Inc., 1985.

Germain, Carel B. and Gitterman, A. *The Life Model of Social Work Practice*. New York: Columbia University Press, 1980.

Getzel, G. "Social Work with Family Caregivers to the Aged," *Social Casework* 62:4, 1981.

Getzel, G. and Mellor, M.J. (Ed.) *Gerontological Social Work Practice in Long Term Care*. New York: The Haworth Press, 1983.

Goldstein, Rose. "Institutionalizing a Spouse: Who is the Client?" *Journal of Geriatric Psychiatry*, Vol. 16, No. 1, 1983.

Greene, R. *Social Work with The Aged and Their Families*. New York: Aldine de Gruyter, 1986.

Hartford, Margaret E. and Parsons, Rebecca. "Group Work with Relatives of Dependent Older Adults," *The Gerontologist*, Vol. 22, No. 4, 1982.

Hooyman, N.R. and Lustbader, W. *Taking Care: Supporting Older People and Their Families*. New York: The Free Press, 1986.

Horowitz, A. "Family Caregiving to the Frail Elderly," *In Annual Review of Gerontology and Geriatrics*. M. P. Lawton and G. Maddox (Eds.) New York: Springer Publishing Co., 1985.

Huttman, E. *Social Services for the Elderly*. New York: The Free Press, 1985.

Johnson, Harriette C. "Emerging Concerns in Family Therapy," *Social Work*. Vol. 31, No. 4, 1986.

Kane, R. and Kane, R. *Assessing the Elderly: A Practical Guide to Measurement*. Lexington, MA: Heath & Co., 1983.

_____. "Alternatives to Institutional Care of the Elderly: Beyond the Dichotomy," *The Gerontologist*, Vol. 20, No. 3, 1980.

Koeske, Gary F. and Koeske, Randi Daimon. "Workload and Burnout: Can Social Support and Perceived Accomplishment Help?" *Social Work*, Vol. 34, No. 3, 1989.

Lowy, L. *Social Work With The Aging: The Challenge and Promise of Later Years*. New York: Harper & Row, 1979.

Mace, N. and Robins, P. *The 36-Hour Day*. Baltimore: The Johns Hopkins University Press, 1981.

McDonald, Patricia Alpough and Haney, Margaret. *Counseling the Older Adult: A Training Manual in Clinical Gerontology*. Lexington, MA: Lexington Books, 1988.

Miller, I. and Solomon, R. "The Development of Group Services for the Elderly," In *Social Work Practice: People and Environments*. Germain, Carel B. (Ed). New York: Columbia University Press, 1979.

Monk, A. "Social Work with the Aged: Principles of Practice," *Social Work*, Vol. 26, No. 1, 1981.

Monk, A. (Ed.). *The Age of Aging*. Buffalo, New York: Prometheus Books, 1979.

Monk, A. (Ed.). *Handbook of Gerontological Services* (2nd Edition). New York: Columbia University Press, 1990.

Neugarten, B. (Ed.) *Middle Age and Aging: A Reader in Social Psychology*. Chicago: The University of Chicago Press, 1968.

Palmore, E. *Social Patterns in Normal Aging*. Durham: Duke University Press, 1981.

Parsons, Ruth J., Hernandez, Santos H. and Jorgensen, James D. "Integrated Practice: A Framework for Problem Solving," *Social Work*, Vol. 33, No. 5, 1988.

Sadovoy, Joel, M.D. and Leszcy, Marlyn, M.D. (Eds.) *Treating the Elderly with Psychotherapy: The Scope of Change in Later Life*. Madison, CT: International Universities Press, Inc., 1987.

Schulman, Susan C. "Psychodynamic Group Therapy with Older Women," *Social Case Work*, Vol. 66, No. 10, 1985.

Schulz, James. *The Economics of Aging*. Belmont: Wadsworth, 1983.

Sherman, E. *Counseling the Aging: An Integrative Approach*. New York: The Free Press, 1981.

Silverstone B. and Burack-Weiss, A. "The Social Work Function in Nursing Homes and Home Care," *Journal of Gerontological Social Work*. Fall/Winter 1982.

Silverstone, B. and Burack-Weiss, A. *Social Work Practice with the Frail Elderly and Their Families: The Auxiliary Function Model*. Springfield, IL: C. Thomas, 1983.

Usdin, G. and Hofling, C. (Ed.). *Aging: The Process and the People*. New York: Brunner/Mazel, 1978.

Weiner, Marcella Bakur, Brod, Albert J., and Snadorsky, Alvin M. *Working with the Aged—Practical Approaches in the Institution and Community* (2nd Ed.). Hormick, CT: Appleton-Century-Crafts, 1987.

Weissman, Celia B. and Schwartz, Paula. "Worker Expectations in Group Work with the Frail Elderly: Modifying the Models for a Better Fit," *Social Work with Groups*, Vol. 12, No. 3, 1989.

Zarit, S. *Aging* and *Mental Disorders*. New York: The Free Press, 1983.

Zohar, J. and Belmaher, R.H. (Eds.). *Treating Resistant Depression*. Great Neck, NY: P.M.A., 1987.

Appendix C

Exercises for Student Group Discussions

The following interchanges are simulations of those that frequently take place between elders and social workers. The responses clearly do not exhaust the range of possibilities. They are merely indicative of what social workers often say.

The objective of this exercise is to stimulate group discussion through role play. This method heightens awareness of the way in which worker responses influence the course of an interview.

I don't know why I go on living. There is nothing left for me.

- No one knows why life goes on. It is in God's hands.
- It sounds as if you're feeling pretty hopeless.
- But you told me just yesterday how much you enjoy bingo.
- I have never seen you look so sad. Has something happened recently to make you feel this way?
- How long have you felt this way?
- What about your situation bothers you the most?
- I am sorry that you are so unhappy, and I'd like to help.
- What do you mean by "nothing left"?

I travelled alot when I was young for my business, and I really enjoyed it. Do you know I even got to China before it went red?

- The Activities Department shows travelogues sometimes. I could find out when, and maybe you could go.
- Then I imagine it must be hard for you now to be so confined here.
- I like to travel too. Last summer I went to Mexico, and next year I'm going to France.

- Do you think about those days often?
  That sounds fascinating. Tell me more about it!
- That's very nice. You see, that is one reason why I am coming to see you, to help you reminisce about happier times.
- What a coincidence. I went to China this summer and have slides. If you like, I could bring them in and we could compare notes on our travels.

Why do I need to see a social worker? I've told my problem to three social workers, and I *still* have a crazy roommate.

- That sounds very frustrating.
- So you're wondering what I can do that they couldn't?
- Well, you see, I want to get to know you to help you with your concerns.
- You sound pretty down on social workers.
- Maybe I won't be any more help, but you seem so upset that I'd sure like to try.
- How is she crazy?
- Perhaps you're wondering why they keep sending social workers to see you when none accomplish anything.
- You must be tired of telling your story over and over again, and nothing changes.
- I'm sure all the social workers did their best, but you see in a big institution like this not everyone can be satisfied.

The young have their own lives. They don't want to be bothered with the old.

- Well, that's not always true. I'm young, and I'm very interested in old people.
- How about the young people in your family?
- It must be hard to feel that you're a bother.
- Perhaps you're wondering why I am interested in you?
- Yes. It is a youth-oriented culture.
- Has something in your own experience led you to that conclusion?

It hurts all the time. See, how hard it is for me to move these fingers? Yesterday, it hurt so much that. . . .

- It must be hard not to be able to do for yourself when, as you told me, you used to be so independent.
- Have you told the nurse about this?
- (Waiting for a pause) Well, that's too bad. What I came to talk about today was your relationship with your daughter.
- Are there other things you used to do that you can't anymore?
- That sounds really terrible. What do you do when you feel like this?

Appendix D

Process Recording
of a First Conference
with a Student

BACKGROUND

J. is placed at a senior center/nutrition site. The center director, not a social worker, is task supervisor. With my direction as to learning needs, she selected three of the cases. One was self-referred. A group for seniors suffering memory loss is in the planning stages.

J., in her early 30s, is a bright, articulate student. Her recording was six tightly-packed pages. Asides in the process were thoughtful and non-defensive. The week's work showed a quick assimilation into the life of the center and an active reaching out to be helpful. The beginner's reliance on instant solutions was evident, as well as premature reassurance that cut off exploration. However, there was also empathy, astute observations, and sensitive responses. On the whole, a promising beginning. J.'s agenda was general — contracting, next steps with clients, help with the group.

THE CONFERENCE

I began by asking J. her overall reaction to the center and assignment. She was enthusiastic about both but quickly directed me back to the work she had done. Recognizing her need for acknowledgement, I briefly commented on the positives. I noted that because of her ease in getting into the work, she was indeed "up to her ears" the very first week. We laughed and then turned to the self-referred case, Mrs. D.

Mrs. D. said, "I have a problem with my sister," then asked for a referral to Medicard for homemaker service. Her sister's demands for care were wearing her out. J. recognized that Mrs. D. was upset about the entire situation. However, she didn't know how to engage her in talking about it, so she made the referral and promised to follow up on it. J. said, "probably I should have told her talking would help. But I'm not sure it would." I told her I was not sure either. J. looked surprised. I said, "Mrs. D. can talk to a lot of people. How would contact with you be different?" J. struggled with this first citing than rejecting her own therapeutic experience, "I'm not her therapist." I reminded her that Mrs. D. began by stating a problem and possible solution, and J. had begun work on it by the referral. What other work could she and Mrs. D. do? J. said it would be good for Mrs. D. to "let off steam." I agreed and added there may be alternative approaches to the sister or other resources — all of which would depend on further exploration. J. asked again about the contract. I explained that it was not yet a contract, rather an offer of service and suggested a role play. J. tried this with alacrity. She tested and rejected many openings ("too vague" or "too long"). When she hit on something good, I said so. ("You told me how hard it is with your sister living in another town." I said, "She will know you really listened to her." J. said, "Yes. I should be specific.")

After she came up with a few good offers, I was ready to move on. However, J. detained me, trying to perfect them. At first, I didn't understand why — I said she didn't have to memorize the words. If she understood the idea, it would come out right. Then she mentioned her fear that Mrs. D. might not accept. I said it was not her responsibility to sell the service, just to offer it. Mrs. D. could accept, reject, or think about it. J. was relieved. (I could have spared myself the guessing game by simply asking J. what bothered her!)

We went on to Mrs. M. a recent widow. J.'s first encounter with her was in a social context. She now had to engage her as a client. The role play showed good progression from Mrs. D. However, I pointed out that Mrs. M., being designated a case by someone else, might well ask "Why me?" J. agreed and role played many convoluted ways of explaining. Neither of us was satisfied. Finally I asked J. why she was referred. J. said that the center director was concerned that Mrs. M. seemed so depressed and lost since her husband died. I wondered if J. could say that. She said she could. I noted that the simplest, most honest statement is generally the best.

Mrs. K. is the only black member of the center and was referred because she was experiencing rejection from the other members. J.'s intervention had been to force Mrs. K. into a bingo game. It had a bad result. My intention was to stick closely to the record. Instead I asked, "Why does she subject herself to this?" J. looked as if a light bulb has gone on. "That's it! I was so involved in making the members accept her, I never considered her side of the situation." She then went on to say that although she knows she must be "more passive and make a space for the client" she is "action overted, wants to give advice and make things better." I recalled that I too had begun thinking I was Joyce Brothers, but it passed. We laughed. She seemed more relaxed. We turned to the record and did a line by line. J. recognized that she had been so eager to show her acceptance of the client that she had not picked up on the feeling expressed. She role played alternatives very well, and I told her so.

The last case, Mrs. P., posed a dilemma for me. All factors pointed to what is commonly known as a chronic schizophrenic personality. I did not want to begin with a label that would obscure the individual personality and functional capacity of the client. I did not wish to alarm the student either. Yet, I could not deny the psychodynamic understanding needed in beginnings with this type of client. I began by asking J. what she thought of the client's history of family suicide, psychiatric hospitalizations, denial of having been married or a mother, erratic job pattern, etc. J. said "extreme." What struck her most was that terrible lost look in Mrs. P.'s eyes. J. would give anything to make it better. She also noted Mrs. P.'s peculiar reaction to her—one day very friendly, the next barely acknowledging her. I said that all this was typical with people who were severely disturbed through most of their lives. I knew she would be studying clinical entities and gave the diagnostic label. She is ultimately interested in being a psychotherapist and will read and learn more about the conflicts within the mental health professions about classifications, etc. However, for our purposes, understanding Mrs. P.'s present problem with trust and relationships was the key. I advised a gentle beginning with no demands. J.'s suggestion of letting Mrs. P. show her the neighborhood (Mrs. P. loves to walk the streets) was great. I said that for Mrs. P. just getting through the day was hard. Anything J. could do to ease this stuggle would be a lift — although the lost look would probably remain.

At the end, we spoke of recruitment for and structure of the group. J. was interested in Poetry and Oral History, and I gave her some references. I also gave her one article on work with the aging that students have found helpful.

In conclusion, I asked how she felt about the week ahead. Any questions? She said that she knew what she was going to do — that she had not realized before what supervision was. She had really liked it. It was evident that she was "up" about her beginnings.

COMMENTS

The conduct of this supervision was evenly divided among discussion, role play, and didactic teaching. J. was such an eager learner that I had to curb my tendency to lecture. Generally, I use a line-by-line reading of the record. However, in this first conference, it seemed less appropriate.

Index